The Writings of Dionysius

The Writings of Dionysius

The Writings of Dionysius

© Lighthouse Publishing 2023

Written by: Dionysius (AD 200 - 265)
Translated by: **Rev. S. D. F. Salmond, M.A.** (1838-1905)
Updated into Modern U.S English: A.M. Overett (b.1960)

All rights reserved. Without limiting the rights under copyright reserved above, no part of this publication may be reproduced, stored in a retrieval system, or transmitted, in any form or by any means (electronic, mechanical, photocopying, recording or otherwise), without the prior written permission of the copyright owner of this book.

Published by
Lighthouse Publishing
SAN 257-4330
228 Freedom Parkway
Hoschton, GA 30548
United States of America

www.lighthousechristianpublishing.com

Introductory Note
to
Dionysius, Bishop of Alexandria.

[a.d. 200–265.] The great Origen had twin children in Gregory and Dionysius. Their lives ran in parallel lines, and are said to have ended on the same day; and nobly did they sustain the dignity and orthodoxy of the pre-eminent school which was soon to see its bright peculiar star in Athanasius. Dionysius is supposed to have been a native of Alexandria, of heathen parentage, and of a family possessed of wealth and honorable rank. Early in life he seems to have been brought under the influence of certain presbyters; and a voice seemed to speak to him in a vision encouraging him to "prove all things, and hold fast that which is good." We find him at the feet of Origen a diligent pupil, and afterward, as a presbyter, succeeding Heraclas (a.d. 232) as the head of the school, sitting in Origen's seat. For about fifteen years he further illuminated this illustrious chair; and then, in ripe years, about a.d. 246, he succeeded Heraclas again as bishop of Alexandria, at that time, beyond all comparison, the greatest and the most powerful See of Christendom.

For a year or two he fed his flock in peace; but then trouble broke in upon his people, even under the kindly reign of Philip. Things grew worse, till under Decius the eighth persecution was let loose throughout the empire. Like Cyprian, Dionysius retired for a season, upon like considerations, but not until he had been arrested and providentially delivered from death in a singular manner. On returning to his work, he found the Church greatly disturbed by the questions concerning the lapsed, with which Cyprian's history has made us acquainted. In the letter to Fabius will be found details of the earlier persecution, and in that against Germanus are interesting facts of his own experience. The Epistle to the Alexandrians contains very full particulars of the pestilence which succeeded these calamities; and it is especially noteworthy as contrasting the humanity and benevolence of Christians with the cruel and cowardly indifference of the pagans towards the dying and the dead. Seditions and tumults followed, on which we have our author's reflections in the Epistle to Hierax, with not a few animated touches of description concerning the condition of Alexandria after such desolations. In the affair of Cyprian with Stephen he stood by the great Carthaginian doctor, and maintained the positions expressed in the letter of Firmilian. Wars, pestilences, and the irruptions of barbarians, make up the history of the residue of the period, through which Dionysius was found a "burning and a shining light" to the Church; his great influence extending throughout the East, and to the West also. I may leave the residue of his story to the introductory remarks of the translator, and to his valuable annotations, to which it will not be necessary for me to add many of my own. But I must find room to express my admiration for his character, which was never found wanting amid many terrible trials of character and of faith itself. His pen was never idle; his learning and knowledge of the Scriptures are apparent, even in the fragments that have come down to us; his fidelity to the traditions received from Origen and Heraclas are not less conspicuous; and in all his dealings with his brethren of the East and West there reigns over his conduct that pure spirit of the Gospel which proves that the virgin-age of the Church was not yet of the past. A beautiful moderation and breadth of sympathy distinguish his episcopal utterances; and, great as was his diocese, he seems equally devoid of prelatic pride and of that wicked ambition which too soon after the martyr-ages proved the bane of the Church's existence. The following is the Translator's Introductory Notice.

For our knowledge of the career of this illustrious disciple of Origen we are indebted chiefly to Eusebius, in the sixth and seventh books of his *Historia Ecclesiastica,* and in the fourteenth book of his *Præparatio Evangelica.* He appears to have been the son of pagan parents; but after studying the doctrines of various of the schools of philosophy, and coming under the influence of Origen, to whom he had attached himself as a pupil, he was led to embrace the Christian faith. This step was taken at an early period, and, as he informs us, only after free examination and careful inquiry into the great systems of heathen belief. He was made a presbyter in Alexandria after this decision; and on the elevation of Heraclas to the bishopric of that city, Dionysius succeeded him in the presidency of the catechetical school there about a.d. 232. After holding that position for some fifteen years Heraclas died, and Dionysius was again chosen to be his successor; and ascending the episcopal throne of Alexandria about a.d. 247 or 248, he retained that See till his death in the year 265. The period of his activity as bishop was a time of great suffering and continuous anxiety; and between the terrors of persecution on the one hand, and the cares of controversy on the other, he found little repose in his office. During the Decian persecution he was arrested and hurried off by the soldiers to a small town named Taposiris, lying between Alexandria and Canopus. But he was rescued from the peril of that seizure in a remarkably providential manner, by a sudden rising of the people of the rural district through which he was carried. Again, however, he was called to suffer, and that more severely, when the persecution under Valerian broke out in the year 257. On making open confession of his faith on this occasion he was banished, at a time when he was seriously ill, to Cephro, a wild and barren district in Libya; and not until he had spent two or three years in exile there was he enabled to return to Alexandria, in virtue of the edict of Gallienus. At various times he had to cope, too, with the miseries of pestilence and famine and civil conflicts in the seat of his bishopric. In the many ecclesiastical difficulties of his age he was also led to take a prominent part. When the keen contest was waged on the subject of the rebaptism of recovered heretics about the year 256, the matter in dispute was referred by both parties to his judgment, and he composed several valuable writings on the question. Then he was induced to enter the lists with the Sabellians, and in the course of a lengthened controversy did much good service against their tenets. The uncompromising energy of his opposition to that sect carried him, however, beyond the bounds of prudence, so that he himself gave expression to opinions not easily reconcilable with the common orthodox doctrine. For these he was called to account by Dionysius bishop of Rome; and when a synod had been summoned to consider the case, he promptly and humbly acknowledged the error into which his precipitate zeal had drawn him. Once more, he was urged to give his help in the difficulty with Paul of Samosata. But as the burden of years and infirmities made it impossible for him to attend the synod convened at Antioch in 265 to deal with that troublesome heresiarch, he sent his opinion on the subject of discussion in a letter to the council, and died soon after, towards the close of the same year. The responsible duties of his bishopric had been discharged with singular faithfulness and patience throughout the seventeen eventful years during which he occupied the office. Among the ancients he was held in the highest esteem both for personal worth and for literary usefulness; and it is related that there was a church dedicated to him in Alexandria. One feature that appears very prominently in his character, is the spirit of independent investigation which possessed him. It was only after candid examination of the current philosophies that he was induced to become a Christian; and after his adoption of the faith, he kept himself abreast of all the controversies of the time, and perused with an impartial mind the works of the great heretics. He acted on this principle through his whole course as a teacher, pronouncing against such writings only when he had made himself familiar with their contents, and saw how to refute them. And we are told in Eusebius, that when a certain presbyter once remonstrated with him on this subject, and warned him of the injury he might do to his own soul by habituating himself to the perusal of these heterodox productions, Dionysius was confirmed in his purpose by a vision and a voice which were sent him, as he thought, from heaven to relieve him of all such fear, and to encourage him to read and prove all that might come into his hand, because that method had been from the very first the cause of faith to him. The moderation of his character, again, is not less worthy of notice. In the case of the Novatian schism, while he was from the first decidedly opposed to the principles of the party, he strove by patient and affectionate argumentation to persuade the leader to submit. So, too, in the disputes on baptism we find him urgently entreating the Roman bishop Stephen not to press matters to extremity with the Eastern Church, nor destroy the peace she had only lately begun to enjoy. Again, in the chiliastic difficulties excited by Nepos, and kept up by Coracion, we see him assembling all the parochial clergy who held these opinions, and inviting all the laymen of the diocese also to attend the conference, and discussing the question for three whole days with all these ministers, considering their arguments, and meeting all their objections patiently by Scripture testimony, until he persuades Coracion himself to retract, and receives the thanks of the pastors, and restores unity of faith in his bishopric. On these occasions his mildness, and benignity, and moderation stand out in bold relief; and on others we trace similar evidence of his broad sympathies and his large and liberal spirit. He was possessed also of a remarkably fertile pen; and the number of his theological writings, both formal treatises and more familiar epistles, was very considerable. All these, however, have perished, with the exception of what Eusebius and other early authors already referred to have preserved. The most important of these compositions are the following: 1. *A Treatise on the Promises,* in two books, which was written against Nepos, and of which Eusebius has introduced two pretty large extracts into the third and seventh books of his *History.* 2. *A Book on Nature,* addressed to Timotheus, in opposition to the Epicureans, of which we have some sections in the *Præpar. Evangel.* of Eusebius. 3. *A Work against the Sabellians,* addressed to Dionysius bishop of Rome, in four books or letters, in which he deals with his own unguarded statements in the controversy with Sabellius, and of which certain portions have come down to us in Athanasius and Basil. In addition to these, we possess a number of his epistles in whole or part, and a few exegetical fragments. There is a Scholium in the Codex Amerbachianus which may be given here:—It should be known that this sainted Dionysius became a hearer of Origen in the fourth year of the reign of Philip, who succeeded Gordian in the empire. On the death of Heraclas, the thirteenth bishop of the church of Alexandria, he was put in possession of the headship of that church; and after a period of seventeen years, embracing the last three years of the reign of Philip, and the one year of that of Decius, and the one year of Gallus and Volusianus the son of Decius, and twelve years of the reigns of Valerian and his son Gallus (Gallienus), he departed to the Lord. And Basilides was bishop of the parishes in the Pentapolis of Libya, as Eusebius informs us in the sixth and seventh books of his *Ecclesiastical History*.

The Works of Dionysius.
Extant Fragments.

Part I.—Containing Various Sections of the Works.

I.—From the Two Books on the Promises.

1. But as they produce a certain composition by Nepos, on which they insist very strongly, as if it demonstrated incontestably that there will be a (temporal) reign of Christ upon the earth, I have to say, that in many other respects I accept the opinion of Nepos, and love him

The Writings of Dionysius

at once for his faith, and his laboriousness, and his patient study in the Scriptures, as also for his great efforts in psalmody, by which even now many of the brethren are In opposition to Noëtus, a bishop in Egypt. Eusebius, *Hist. Eccl.*, vii. 24 and 25. Eusebius introduces this extract in the following terms: "There are also two books of his on the subject of the promises. The occasion of writing these was furnished by a certain Nepos, a bishop in Egypt, who taught that the promises which were given to holy men in the sacred Scriptures were to be understood according to the Jewish sense of the same; and affirmed that there would be some kind of a millennial period, plenished with corporeal delights, upon this earth. And as he thought that he could establish this opinion of his by the Revelation of John, he had composed a book on this question, entitled *Refutation of the Allegorists*. This, therefore, is sharply attacked by Dionysius in his books on the Promises. And in the first of these books he states his own opinion on the subject; while in the second he gives us a discussion on the Revelation of John, in the introduction to which he makes mention of Nepos." [Of this Noëtus, see the *Philosophumena*, vol. v., this series.]

As it is clear from this passage that this work by Dionysius was written against Nepos, it is strange that, in his preface to the eighteenth book of his Commentaries on Isaiah, Jerome should affirm it to have been composed against Irenæus of Lyons. Irenæus was certainly of the number of those who held millennial views, and who had been persuaded to embrace such by Papias, as Jerome himself tells us in the *Catalogus* and as Eusebius explains towards the close of the third book of his *History*. But that this book by Dionysus was written not against Irenæus but against Nepos, is evident, not only from this passage in Eusebius, but also from Jerome himself, in his work *On Ecclesiastical Writers*, where he speaks of Dionysius.—Vales. [Compare (this series, *infra*) the comments of Victorinus of Petau for a Western view of the millennial subject.] τῆς πολλῆς ψαλμῳδίας. Christophorsonus interprets this of psalms and hymns composed by Nepos. It was certainly the practice among the ancient Christians to compose psalms and hymns in honor of Christ. Eusebius bears witness to this in the end of the fifth book of his *History*. Mention is made of these psalms in the Epistle of the Council of Antioch against Paul of Samosata, and in the penultimate canon of the Council of Laodicea, where there is a clear prohibition of the use of ψαλμοὶ ἰδιωτικοί in the church, i.e., of psalms composed by private individuals. For this custom had obtained great prevalence, so that many persons composed psalms in honor of Christ, and got them sung in the church. It is psalms of this kind, consequently, that the Fathers of the Council of Laodicea forbid to be sung thereafter in the church, designating them ἰδιωτικοί, i.e., composed delighted. I hold the man, too, in deep respect still more, inasmuch as he has gone to his rest before us. Nevertheless the truth is to be prized and reverenced above all things else. And while it is indeed proper to praise and approve ungrudgingly anything that is said aright, it is no less proper to examine and correct anything which may appear to have been written unsoundly. If he had been present then himself, and had been stating his opinions orally, it would have been sufficient to discuss the question together without the use of writing, and to endeavor to convince the opponents, and carry them along by interrogation and reply. But the work is published, and is, as it seems to some, of a very persuasive character; and there are unquestionably some teachers, who hold that the law and the prophets are of no importance, and who decline to follow the Gospels, and who depreciate the epistles of the apostles, and who have also made large promises regarding the doctrine of this composition, as though it were some great and hidden mystery, and who, at the same time, do not allow that our simpler brethren have any sublime and elevated conceptions either of our Lord's appearing in His glory and His true divinity, or of our own resurrection from the dead, and of our being gathered together to Him, and assimilated to Him, but, on the contrary, endeavor to lead them to hope for things which are trivial and corruptible, and only such as what we find at present in the kingdom of God. And since this is the case, it becomes necessary for us to discuss this subject with our brother Nepos just as if he were present.

2. *After certain other matters, he adds the following statement:*—Being then in the Arsinoitic prefecture—where, as you are aware, this doctrine was current long ago, and caused such division, that schisms and apostasies took place in whole churches—I called together the presbyters and the teachers among the brethren in the villages, and those of the brethren also who wished to attend were present. I exhorted them to make an investigation into that dogma in public. Accordingly, when they had brought this book before us, as though it were a kind of weapon or impregnable battlement, I sat with them for three days in succession from morning till evening, and attempted to set them right on the subjects propounded in the composition. Then, too, I was greatly gratified by observing the constancy of the brethren, and their love of the truth, and their docility and intelligence, as we proceeded, in an orderly method, and

in a spirit of moderation, to deal with questions, and difficulties, and concessions. For we took care not to press, in every way and with jealous urgency, opinions which had once been adopted, even though they might appear to be correct. Neither did we evade objections alleged by others; but we endeavored as far as possible to keep by the subject in hand, and to establish the positions pertinent to it. Nor, again, were we ashamed to change our opinions, if reason convinced us, and to acknowledge the fact; but rather with a good conscience, and in all sincerity, and with open hearts before God, we accepted all that could be established by the demonstrations and teachings of the Holy Scriptures. And at last the author and introducer of this doctrine, whose name was Coracion, in the hearing of all the brethren present, made acknowledgment of his position, and engaged to us that he would no longer hold by his opinion, nor discuss it, nor mention it, nor teach it, as he had been completely convinced by the arguments of those opposed to it. The rest of the brethren, also, who were present, were delighted with the conference, and with the conciliatory spirit and the harmony exhibited by all.

3. *Then, a little further on, he speaks of the Revelation of John as follows*:—Now some before our time have set aside this book, and repudiated it entirely, criticizing it chapter by chapter, and endeavoring to show it to be without either sense or reason. They have alleged also that its title is false; for they deny that John is the author. Nay, further, they hold that it can be no sort of revelation, because it is covered with so gross and dense a veil of ignorance. They affirm, therefore, that none of the apostles, nor indeed any of the saints, nor any person belonging to the Church, could be its author; but that Cerinthus, and

the heretical sect founded by him, and named after him the Cerinthian sect, being desirous of attaching the authority of a great name to the fiction propounded by him, prefixed that title to the book. For the doctrine inculcated by Cerinthus is this: that there will be an earthly reign of Christ; and as he was himself a man devoted to the pleasures of the body, and altogether carnal in his dispositions, he fancied that that kingdom would consist in those kinds of gratifications on which his own heart was set,—to wit, in the delights of the belly, and what comes beneath the belly, that is to say, in eating and drinking, and marrying, and in other things under the guise of which he thought he could indulge his appetites with a better grace, such as festivals, and sacrifices, and the slaying of victims. But I, for my part, could not venture to set this book aside, for there are many brethren who value it highly. Yet, having formed an idea of it as a composition exceeding my capacity of understanding, I regard it as containing a kind of hidden and wonderful intelligence on the several subjects which come under it. For though I cannot comprehend it, I still suspect that there is some deeper sense underlying the words. And I do not measure and judge its expressions by the standard of my own reason, but, making more allowance for faith, I have simply regarded them as too lofty for my comprehension; and I do not forthwith reject what I do not understand, but I am only the more filled with wonder at it, in that I have not been able to discern its import.

4. *After this, he examines the whole book of the Revelation; and having proved that it cannot possibly be understood according to the bald, literal sense, he proceeds thus:*—When the prophet now has completed, so to speak, the whole prophecy, he pronounces those blessed

who should observe it, and names himself, too, in the number of the same: "For blessed," says he, "is he that kept the words of the prophecy of this book; and I John *who* saw and heard these things." That this person was called John, therefore, and that this was the writing of a John, I do not deny. And I admit further, that it was also the work of some holy and inspired man. But I could not so easily admit that this was the apostle, the son of Zebedee, the brother of James, and the same person with him who wrote the Gospel which bears the title *according to John*, and the catholic epistle. But from the character of both, and the forms of expression, and the whole disposition and execution of the book, I draw the conclusion that the authorship is not his. For the evangelist nowhere else subjoins his name, and he never proclaims himself either in the Gospel or in the epistle.

And a little further on he adds:—John, moreover, nowhere gives us the name, whether as of himself directly (in the first person), or as of another (in the third person). But the writer of the Revelation puts himself forward at once in the very beginning, for he says: "The Revelation of Jesus Christ, which He gave to him to show to His servants quickly; and He sent and signified it by His angel to His servant John, who bare record of the Word of God, and of his testimony, and of all things that he saw." And then he writes also an epistle, in which he says: "John to the seven churches which are in Asia, grace be unto you, and peace." The evangelist, on the other hand, has not prefixed his name even to the catholic epistle; but without any circumlocution, he has commenced at once with the mystery of the divine revelation itself in these terms: "That which was from the beginning, which we have heard, which we have seen with our eyes." And on the ground of such a revelation as that the Lord pronounced Peter blessed, when He said: "Blessed art thou, Simon Bar-jona; for flesh and blood hath not revealed it unto thee, but my Father which is in heaven." And again in the second epistle, which is ascribed to John, the apostle, and in the third, though they are indeed brief, John is not set before us by name; but we find simply the an- onymous writing, "The elder." This other author, on the contrary, did not even deem it sufficient to name himself once, and then to proceed with his narrative; but he takes up his name again, and says: "I John, who also am your brother and companion in tribulation, and in the kingdom and patience of Jesus Christ, was in the isle that is called Patmos for the Word of God, and for the testimony of Jesus Christ." And likewise toward the end he speaks thus: "Blessed is he that kept the sayings of the prophecy of this book; and I John *who* saw these things and heard them." That it is a John, then, that writes these things we must believe, for he himself tells us.

5. What John this is, however, is uncertain. For he has not said, as he often does in the Gospel, that he is the disciple beloved by the Lord, or the one that leaned on His bosom, or the brother of James, or one that was privileged to see and hear the Lord. And surely he would have given us some of these indications if it had been his purpose to make himself clearly known. But of all this he offers us nothing; and he only calls himself our brother and companion, and the witness of Jesus, and one blessed with the seeing and hearing of these revelations. I am also of opinion that there were many persons of the same name with John the apostle, who by their love for him, and their admiration and emulation of him, and their desire to be

loved by the Lord as he was loved, were induced to embrace also the same designation, just as we find many of the children of the faithful called by the names of Paul and Peter. There is, besides, another John mentioned in the Acts of the Apostles, with the surname Mark, whom Barnabas and Paul attached to themselves as companion, and of whom again it is said: "And they had also John to their minister." But whether this is the one who wrote the Revelation, I could not say. For it is not written that he came with them into Asia. But the writer says: "Now when Paul and his company loosed from Paphos, they came to Perga in Pamphylia: and John, departing from them, returned to Jerusalem." I think, therefore, that it was some other one of those who were in Asia. For it is said that there were two monuments in Ephesus, and that each of these bears the name of John.

6. And from the ideas, and the expressions, and the collocation of the same, it may be very reasonably conjectured that this one is distinct from that. For the Gospel and the Epistle agree with each other, and both commence in the same way. For the one opens thus, "In the beginning was the Word;" while the other opens thus, "That which was from the beginning." The one says: "And the Word was made flesh, and dwelt among us; and we beheld His glory, the glory as of the Only-begotten of the Father." The other says the same things, with a slight alteration: "That which we have heard, which we have seen with our eyes, which we have looked upon, and our hands have handled, of the Word of life: and the life was manifested." For these things are introduced by way of prelude, and in opposition, as he has shown in the subsequent parts, to those who deny that the Lord is come in the flesh. For which reason he has also been careful to

add these words: "And that which we have seen we testify, and show unto you that eternal life which was with the Father, and was manifested unto us: that which we have seen and heard declare we unto you." Thus he keeps to himself, and does not diverge inconsistently from his subjects, but goes through them all under the same heads and in the same phraseologies, some of which we shall briefly mention. Thus the attentive reader will find the phrases, "the life," "the light," occurring often in both; and also such expressions as *fleeing from darkness, holding the truth, grace, joy, the flesh and the blood of the Lord, the judgment, the remission of sins, the love of God toward us, the commandment of love on our side toward each other; as also, that we ought to keep all the commandments, the conviction of the world, of the devil, of Antichrist, the promise of the Holy Spirit, the adoption of God, the faith* required of us in all things, *the Father and the Son*, named as such everywhere. And altogether, through their whole course, it will be evident that the Gospel and the Epistle are distinguished by one and the same character of writing. But the Revelation is totally different, and altogether distinct from this; and I might almost say that it does not even come near it, or border upon it. Neither does it contain a syllable in common with these other books. Nay more, the Epistle—for I say nothing of the Gospel—does not make any mention or evince any notion of the Revelation and the Revelation, in like manner, gives no note of the Epistle. Whereas Paul gives some indication of his revelations in his epistles; which revelations, however, he has not recorded in writing by themselves.

7. And furthermore, on the ground of difference in diction, it is possible to prove a distinction between

the Gospel and the Epistle on the one hand, and the Revelation on the other. For the former are written not only without actual error as regards the Greek language, but also with the greatest elegance, both in their expressions and in their reasonings, and in the whole structure of their style. They are very far indeed from betraying any barbarism or solecism, or any sort of vulgarism, in their diction. For, as might be presumed, the writer possessed the gift of both kinds of discourse, the Lord having bestowed both these capacities upon him, viz., that of knowledge and that of expression. That the author of the latter, however, saw a revelation, and received knowledge and prophecy, I do not deny. Only I perceive that his dialect and language are not of the exact Greek type, and that he employs barbarous idioms, and in some places also solecisms. These, however, we are under no necessity of seeking out at present. And I would not have any one suppose that I have said these things in the spirit of ridicule; for I have done so only with the purpose of setting right this matter of the dissimilarity subsisting between these writings.

II. From the Books on Nature.

I. In Opposition to Those of the School of Epicurus Who Deny the Existence of a Providence, and Refer the Constitution of the Universe to Atomic Bodies.

Is the universe one coherent whole, as it seems to be in our own judgment, as well as in that of the wisest of the Greek philosophers, such as Plato and Pythagoras, and the Stoics and Heraclitus? or is it a duality, as some may possibly have conjectured? or is it indeed something manifold and infinite, as has been the opinion of certain others who, with a variety of mad speculations and fanciful usages of terms, have sought to divide and resolve the essential matter of the universe, and lay down the position that it is infinite and unoriginated, and without the sway of Providence? For there are those who, giving the name of atoms to certain imperishable and most minute bodies which are supposed to be infinite in number, and positing also the existence of a certain vacant space of an unlimited vastness, allege that these atoms, as they are borne along casually in the void, and clash all fortuitously against each other in an unregulated whirl, and become commingled one with another in a multitude of forms, enter into combination with each other, and thus gradually form this world and all objects in it; yea, more, that they construct infinite worlds. This was the opinion of Epicurus and Democritus; only they differed in one point, in so far as the former supposed these atoms to be all most minute and consequently imperceptible, while Democritus held that there were also some among them of a very large size. But they both hold that such atoms do exist, and that they are so called on account of their indissoluble consistency. There are some, again, who give the name of atoms to certain bodies which are indivisible into parts, while they are themselves parts of the universe, out of which in their undivided state all things are made up, and into which they are dissolved again. And the allegation is, that Diodorus was the person who gave them their names as bodies indivisible into parts. But it is also said that Heraclides attached another name to them, and called them "weights;" and from him the physician Asclepiades also derived that name.

II. A Refutation of This Dogma on the Ground of Familiar Human Analogies.

How, shall we bear with these men who assert that all those wise, and consequently also noble, constructions (in the universe) are only the works of common chance? those objects, I mean, of which each taken by itself as it is made, and the whole system collectively, were seen to be good by Him by whose command they came into existence. For, as it is said, "God saw everything that He had made, and, behold, it was very good." But truly these men do not reflect on[648] the analogies even of small familiar things which might come under their observation at any time, and from which they might learn that no object of any utility, and fitted to be serviceable, is made without design or by mere chance, but is wrought by skill of hand, and is contrived so as to meet its proper use. And when the object falls out of service and becomes useless, then it also begins to break up indeterminately, and to decom- pose and dissipate its materials in every casual and unregulated way, just as the wisdom by which it was skillfully constructed at first no longer controls and maintains it. For a cloak, for example, cannot be made without the weaver, as if the warp could be set aright and the woof could be entwined with it by their own spontaneous action; while, on the other hand, if it is once worn out, its tattered rags are flung aside. Again, when a house or a city is built, it does not take on its stones, as if some of them placed themselves spontaneously upon the foundations, and others lifted themselves up on the several layers, but the builder carefully disposes the skillfully prepared stones in their proper positions; while if the structure happens once to give way, the stones are separated and cast down and scattered about. And so, too, when a ship is built, the keel does not lay itself, neither does the mast erect itself in the center, nor do all the other timbers take up their positions casually and by their own motion. Nor, again, do the so-called hundred beams in the wain fit themselves spontaneously to the vacant spaces they severally light on. But the carpenter in both cases puts the materials together in the right way and at the right time. And if the ship goes to sea and is wrecked, or if the wain drives along on land and is shattered, their timbers are broken up and cast abroad anywhere,—those of the former by the waves, and those of the latter by the violence of the impetus. In like manner, then, we might with all propriety say also to these men, that those atoms of theirs, which remain idle and unmanipulated and useless, are introduced vainly. Let them, accordingly, seek for themselves to see into what is beyond the reach of sight, and conceive what is beyond the range of conception; unlike him who in these terms confesses to God that things like these had been shown him only by God Himself: "Mine eyes did see Thy work, being till then imperfect." But when they assert now that all those things of grace and beauty, which they declare to be textures finely wrought out of atoms, are fabricated spontaneously by these bodies without either wisdom or perception in them, who can endure to hear them talk in such terms of those unregulated atoms, than which even the spider, that plies its proper craft of itself, is gifted with more sagacity?

III. A Refutation on the Ground of the Constitution of the Universe.

Or who can bear to hear it maintained, that this mighty habitation, which is constituted of heaven and earth, and which is called "Cosmos" on account of the magnitude and the plenitude of the wisdom which has been brought to bear upon it, has been established in all its order and beauty by those atoms which hold their course devoid of order and beauty, and that that same state of disorder has grown into this true Cosmos, Order? Or who can believe that those regular movements and courses are the products of a certain unregulated impetus? Or who can allow that the perfect concord subsisting among the celestial bodies derives its harmony from instruments destitute both of concord and harmony? Or, again, if there is but one and the same substance in all things, and if there is the same incorruptible nature in all,—the only elements of difference being, as they aver, size and figure,—how comes it that there are some bodies divine and perfect, and eternal, as they would phrase it, or lasting, as someone may prefer to express it; and among these some, that are visible and others that are invisible,—the visible including such as sun, and moon, and stars, and earth, and water; and the invisible including gods, and demons, and spirits? For the existence of such they cannot possibly deny however desirous to do so. And again, there are other objects that are long-lived, both animals and plants. As to animals, there are, for example, among birds, as they say, the eagle, the raven, and the phoenix; and among creatures living on land, there are the stag, and the elephant, and the dragon; and among aquatic creatures there are the whales, and such like monsters of the deep. And as to trees, there are the palm, and the oak, and the persea; and among trees, too, there are some that are evergreens, of which kind fourteen have been reckoned up by someone; and there are others that only bloom for a certain season, and then shed their leaves. And there are other objects, again—which indeed constitute the vast mass of all which either grow or are begotten—that have an early death and a brief life. And among these is man himself, as a certain holy scripture says of him: "Man that is born of woman is of few days." Well, but I suppose they will reply that the varying conjunctions of the atoms account fully for differences so great in the matter of duration. For it is maintained that there are some things that are compressed together by them, and firmly interlaced, so that they become closely compacted bodies, and consequently exceedingly hard to break up; while there are others in which more or less the conjunction of the atoms is of a looser and weaker nature, so that either quickly or after some time they separate themselves from their orderly constitution. And, again, there are some bodies made up of atoms of a definite kind and a certain common figure, while there are others made up of diverse atoms diversely disposed. But who, then, is the sagacious discriminator, that brings certain atoms into collocation, and separates others; and marshals some in such wise as to form the sun, and others in such a way as to originate the moon, and adapts all in natural fitness, and in accordance with the proper constitution of each star? For surely neither would those solar atoms, with their peculiar size and kind, and with their special mode of collocation, ever have reduced themselves so as to effect the production of a moon; nor, on the other hand, would the conjunctions of these lunar atoms ever have developed into a sun. And as certainly neither would Arcturus, resplendent as he is, ever boast his having the atoms possessed by Lucifer, nor would the Pleiades glory in being constituted of those of Orion. For well has Paul expressed the distinction when he says: "There is one glory of the sun, and another glory of the moon, and another glory of the stars: for one star differed from another star in glory." And if the coalition effected among them has been an unintelligent one, as is the case with soulless objects, then they must needs have had some sagacious artificer; and if their union has been one without the determination of will, and only of necessity, as is the case with irrational objects, then some skillful leader must have brought them together and taken them under his charge. And if they have linked themselves together spontaneously, for a spontaneous work, then some admirable architect must have apportioned their work for them, and assumed the superintendence among them; or there must have been one to do with them as the general does who loves order and discipline, and who does not leave his army in an irregular condition, or suffer all things to go on confusedly, but marshals the cavalry in their proper succession, and disposes the heavy-armed infantry in their due array, and the javelin-men by themselves, and the archers separately, and the slingers in like manner, and sets each force in its appropriate position, in order that all those equipped in the same way may engage together. But if these teachers think that this illustration is but a joke, because I institute a comparison between very large bodies and very small, we may pass to the very smallest.

Then we have what follows:—But if neither the word, nor the choice, nor the order of a ruler is laid upon them, and if by their own act they keep themselves right in the vast com- motion of the stream in which they move, and convey themselves safely through the mighty uproar of the collisions, and if like atoms meet and group themselves with like, not as being brought together by God, according to the poet's fancy, but rather as naturally recognizing the affinities subsisting between each other, then truly we have here a most marvelous democracy of atoms, wherein friends welcome and embrace friends, and all are eager to sojourn together in one domicile; while some by their own determination have rounded themselves off into that mighty luminary the sun, so as to make day; and others have formed themselves into many pyramids of blazing stars, it may be, so as to crown also the whole heavens; and others have reduced themselves into the circular figure, so as to impart a certain solidity to the ether, and arch it over, and constitute it a vast graduated ascent of luminaries, with this object also, that the various conventions of the commoner atoms may select settlements for themselves, and portion out the sky among them for their habitations and stations.

Then, after certain other matters, the discourse proceeds thus:—But inconsiderate men do not see even things that are apparent, and certainly they are far from being cognizant of things that are unapparent. For they do not seem even to have any notion of those regulated risings and settings of the heavenly bodies,—those of the sun, with all their wondrous glory, no less than those of the others; nor do they appear to make due application of the aids furnished through these to men, such as the day that rises clear for man's work, and the night that overshadows earth for man's rest. "For man," it is said, "goes forth unto his work, and to his labor, until the evening." Neither do they consider that other revolution, by which the sun makes out for us determinate times, and convenient seasons, and regular successions, directed by those atoms of which it consists. But even though men like these—and miserable men they are, however they may believe themselves to be righteous—may choose not to admit it, there is a mighty Lord that made the sun, and gave it the impetus for its course by His words. O ye blind ones, do these atoms of yours bring you the winter season and the rains, in order that the earth may yield food for you, and for all creatures living on it? Do they introduce summertime, too, in order that ye may gather their fruits from the trees for your enjoyment? And why, then, do ye not worship these atoms, and offer sacrifices to them as the guardians of earth's fruits? Thankless surely are ye, in not setting solemnly apart for them even the most scanty first fruits of that abundant bounty which ye receive from them.

After a short break he proceeds thus:—Moreover, those stars which form a community so multitudinous and various, which these erratic and ever self-dispersing atoms have constituted, have marked off by a kind of covenant the tracts for their several possessions, portioning these out like colonies and governments, but without the presidency of any founder or house-master; and with pledged fealty and in peace they respect the laws of vicinity with their neighbors, and abstain from passing beyond the boundaries which they received at the outset, just as if they enjoyed the legislative administration of true princes in the atoms. Nevertheless, these atoms exercise no rule. For how could these, that are themselves nothing, do that? But listen to the divine oracles: "The works of the Lord are in judgment; from the beginning, and from His making of them, He disposed the parts thereof. He garnished His works forever, and their principles unto their generations."

Again, after a little, he proceeds thus:—Or what phalanx ever traversed the plain in such perfect order, no trooper outmarching the others, or falling out of rank, or obstructing the course, or suffering himself to be distanced by his comrades in the array, as is the case with that steady advance in regular file, as it were, and with close-set shields, which is presented by this serried and unbroken and undisturbed and unobstructed progress of the hosts of the stars? Albeit by side inclinations and flank movements certain of their revolutions become less clear. Yet, however that may be, they assuredly always keep their appointed periods, and again bear onward determinately to the positions from which they have severally risen, as if they made that their deliberate study. Wherefore let these notable anatomizers of atoms, these dividers of the indivisible, these compounders of the uncompoundable, these adepts in the apprehension of the infinite, tell us whence comes this circular march and course of the heavenly bodies, in which it is not any single combination of atoms that merely chances all unexpectedly to swing itself round in this way; but it is one vast circular choir that moves thus, ever equally and concordantly, and whirls in these orbits. And whence comes it that this mighty multitude of fellow-travelers, all unmarshalled by any captain, all ungifted with any determination of will, and all unendowed with any knowledge of each other, have nevertheless held their course in perfect harmony? Surely, well has the prophet ranked this matter among things which are impossible and undemonstrable,—namely, that two strangers should walk together. For he says, "Shall two come to the same lodging unless they know each other?"

IV. A Refutation of the Same on the Grounds of the Human Constitution.

Further, those men understand neither themselves nor what is proper to themselves. For if any of the leaders in this impious doctrine only considered what manner of person he is himself, and whence he comes, he would surely be led to a wise decision, like one who has obtained understanding of himself, and would say, not to these atoms, but to his Father and Maker, "Thy hands have made me and fashioned me." And he would take up, too, this wonderful account of his formation as it has been given by one of old: "Hast Thou not poured me out as milk, and curdled me as cheese? Thou hast clothed me with skin and flesh, and hast fenced me with bones and sinews. Thou hast granted me life and favor, and Thy visitation hath preserved my spirit." For of what quantity and of what origin were the atoms which the father of Epicurus gave forth from himself when he begat Epicurus? And how, when they were received within his mother's womb, did they coalesce, and take form and figure? and how were they put in motion and made to increase? And how did that little seed of generation draw together the many atoms that were to constitute Epicurus, and change some of them into skin and flesh for a covering, and make bone of others for erectness and strength, and form sinews of others for compact contexture? And how did it frame and adapt the many other members and parts—heart and bowels, and organs of sense, some within and some without—by which the body is made a thing of life? For of all these things there is not one either idle or useless: not even the meanest of them—the hair, or the nails, or such like—is so; but all have their service to do, and all their contribution to make, some of them to the soundness of bodily constitution, and others of them to beauty of appearance. For Providence cares not only for the useful, but also for the seasonable and beautiful. Thus the hair is a kind of protection and covering for the whole head, and the beard is a seemly ornament for the philosopher. It was Providence, then, that formed the constitution of the whole body of man, in all its necessary parts, and imposed on all its members their due connection with each other, and measured out for them their liberal supplies from the universal resources. And the most prominent of these show clearly, even to the uninstructed, by the proof of personal experience, the value and service attaching to them: the head, for example, in the position of supremacy, and the senses set like a guard about the brain, as the ruler in the citadel; and the advancing eyes, and the reporting ears; and the taste which, as it were, is the tribute-gatherer; and the smell, which tracks and searches out its objects: and the touch, which manipulates all put under it.

Hence we shall only run over in a summary way, at present, some few of the works of an all-wise Providence; and after a little we shall, if God grant it, go over them more minutely, when we direct our discourse toward one who has the repute of greater learning. *So*, then, we have the ministry of the hands, by which all kinds of works are wrought, and all skillful professions practiced, and which have all their various faculties furnished them, with a view to the discharge of one common function; and we have the shoulders, with their capacity for bearing burdens; and the fingers, with their power of grasping; and the elbows, with their faculty of bending, by which they can turn inwardly, upon the body, or take an outward inclination, so as to be able either to draw objects toward the body, or to thrust them away from it. We have also the service of the feet, by which the whole terrestrial creation is made to come under our power, the earth itself is traversed thereby, the sea is made navigable, the rivers are crossed, and intercourse is established for all with all things. The belly, too, is the storehouse of meats, with all its parts arranged in their proper collocations, so that it apportions for itself the right measure of aliment, and ejects what is over and above that. And so is it with all the other things by which manifestly the due administration of the constitution of man is wisely secured. Of all these, the intelligent and the unintelligent alike enjoy the same use; but they have not the same comprehension of them. For there are some who refer this whole economy to a power which they conceive to be a true divinity, and which they apprehend as at once the highest intelligence in all things, and the best benefactor to themselves, believing that this economy is all the work of a wisdom and a might which are superior to every other, and in themselves truly divine. And there are others who aimlessly attribute this whole structure of most marvelous beauty to chance and fortuitous coincidence. And in addition to these, there are also certain physicians, who, having made a more effective examination into all these things, and having investigated with utmost accuracy the disposition of the inward parts in especial, have been struck with astonishment at the results of their inquiry, and have been led to deify nature itself. The notions of these men we shall review afterwards, as far as we may be able, though we may only touch the surface of the subject. Meantime, to deal with this matter generally and summarily, let me ask who constructed this whole tabernacle of ours, so lofty, erect, graceful, sensitive, mobile, active, and apt for all things? Was it, as they say, the irrational multitude of atoms? Nay, these, by their conjunctions, could not mold even an image of clay, neither could they hew and polish a statue of stone; nor could they cast and finish an idol of silver or gold; but arts and handicrafts calculated for such operations have been discovered by men who fabricate these objects. And if, even in these, representations and models cannot be made without the aid of wisdom, how can the genuine and original patterns of these copies have come into existence spontaneously? And whence have come the soul, and the intelligence, and the reason, which are born with the philosopher? Has he gathered these from those atoms which are destitute alike of soul, and intelligence, and reason? and has each of these atoms inspired him with some appropriate conception and notion? And are we to suppose that the wisdom of man was made up by these atoms, as the myth of Hesiod tells us that Pandora was fashioned by the gods? Then shall the Greeks have, to give up speaking of the various species of poetry, and music, and astronomy, and geometry, and all the other arts and sciences, as the inventions and instructions of the gods, and shall have to allow that these atoms are the only muses with skill and wisdom for all subjects. For this theogony, constructed of atoms by Epicurus, is indeed something extraneous to the infinite worlds of order, and finds its refuge in the infinite disorder.

V. That to Work is Not a Matter of Pain and Weariness to God.

Now to work, and administer, and do good, and exercise care, and such like actions, may perhaps be hard tasks for the idle, and silly, and weak, and wicked; in whose number truly Epicurus reckons himself, when he propounds such notions about the gods. But to the earnest, and powerful, and intelligent, and prudent, such as philosophers ought to be—and how much more so, therefore, the gods!—these things are not only not disagreeable and irksome, but ever the most delightful, and by far the most welcome of all. To persons of this character, negligence and procrastination in the doing of what is good are a reproach, as the poet admonishes them in these words of counsel:—

"Delay not aught till the morrow."

And then he adds this further sentence of threatening:—

"The lazy procrastinator is ever wrestling with miseries."

And the prophet teaches us the same lesson in a more solemn fashion, and declares that deeds done according to the standard of virtue are truly worthy of God, and that the man who gives no heed to these is accursed: "For cursed be he that doeth the works of the Lord carelessly." Moreover, those who are unversed in any art, and unable to prosecute it perfectly, feel it to be wearisome when they make their first attempts in it, just by reason of the novelty of their experience, and their want of practice in the works. But those, on the other hand, who have made some advance, and much more those who are perfectly trained in the art, accomplish easily and successfully the objects of their labors, and have great pleasure in the work, and would choose rather thus, in the discharge of the pursuits to which they are accustomed, to finish and carry perfectly out what their efforts aim at, than to be made masters of all those things which are reckoned advantageous among men. Yea, Democritus himself, as it is reported, averred that he would prefer the discovery of one true cause to being put in possession of the kingdom of Persia. And that was the declaration of a man who had only a vain and groundless conception of the causes of things, inasmuch as he started with an unfounded principle, and an erroneous hypothesis, and did not discern the real root and the common *law of* necessity in the constitution of natural things, and held as the greatest wisdom the apprehension of things that come about simply in an unintelligent and random way, and set up chance as the mistress and queen of things universal, and even things divine, and endeavored to demonstrate that all things happen by the determination of the same, although at the same time he kept it outside the sphere of the life of men, and convicted those of senselessness who worshipped it. At any rate, at the very beginning of his *Precepts,* he speaks thus: "Men have made an image of chance, as a cover for their own lack of knowledge. For intellect and chance are in their very nature antagonistic to each other. And men have maintained that this greatest adversary to intelligence is its sovereign. Yea, rather, they completely subvert and do away with the one, while they establish the other in its place. For they do not celebrate intelligence as the fortunate, but they laud chance as the most intelligent." Moreover, those who attend to things conducing to the good of life, take special pleasure in what serves the interests of those of the same race with themselves, and seek the recompense of praise and glory in return for labors undertaken in behalf of the general good; while some exert themselves as purveyors of ways and means, others as magistrates, others as physicians, others as statesmen; and even philosophers pride themselves greatly in their efforts after the education of men. Will, then, Epicurus or Democritus be bold enough to assert that in the exertion of philosophizing, they only cause distress to themselves? Nay, rather they will reckon this a pleasure of mind second to none. For even though they maintain the opinion that the good is pleasure, they will be ashamed to deny that philosophizing is the greater pleasure to them. But as to the gods, of whom the poets among them sing that they are the "bestowers of good gifts," these philosophers scoffingly celebrate them in strains like these: "The gods are neither the bestowers nor the sharers in any good thing." And in what manner, forsooth, can they demonstrate that there are gods at all, when they neither perceive their presence, nor discern them as the doers of aught, wherein, indeed, they resemble those who, in their admiration and wonder at the sun and the moon and the stars, have held these to have been named *gods*, from their *running* such courses: when, further, they do not attribute to them any function or power of operation, so as to hold them gods from their *constituting*, that is, from their *making* objects, for thereby in all truth the one maker and operator of all things must be God: and when, in fine, they do not set forth any administration, or judgment, or beneficence of theirs in relation to men, so that we might be bound either by fear or by reverence to worship them? Has Epicurus then been able, forsooth, to see beyond this world, and to overpass the precincts of heaven? or has he gone forth by some secret gates known to himself alone, and thus obtained sight of the gods in the void? and, deeming them blessed in their full felicity, and then becoming himself a passionate aspirant after such pleasure, and an ardent scholar in that life which they pursue in the void, does he now call upon all to participate in this felicity, and urge them thus to make themselves like the gods, preparing as their true *symposium* of blessedness neither heaven nor Olympus, as the poets feign, but the sheer void, and setting before them the ambrosia of atoms, and pledging them in nectar made of the same? However, in matters which have no relation to us, he introduces into his books a myriad oaths and solemn asseverations, swearing constantly both negatively and affirmatively by Jove, and making those whom he meets, and with whom he discusses his doctrines, swear also by the gods, not certainly that he fears them himself, or has any dread of perjury, but that he pronounces all this to be vain, and false, and idle, and unintelligible, and uses it simply as a kind of accompaniment to his words, just as he might also clear his throat, or spit, or twist his face, or move his hand. So completely senseless and empty a pretense was this whole matter of the naming of the gods, in his estimation. But this is also a very patent fact, that, being in fear of the Athenians after (the warning of) the death of Socrates, and being desirous of preventing his being taken for what he really was—an atheist—the subtle charlatan invented for them certain empty shadows of unsubstantial gods. But never surely did he look up to heaven with eyes of true intelligence, so as to hear the clear voice from above, which another attentive spectator did hear, and of which he testified when he said, "The heavens declare the glory of God, and the firmament showed His handiwork." And never surely did he look down upon the world's surface with due reflection; for then would he have learned that "the earth is full of the goodness of the Lord" and that "the earth is the Lord's, and the fulness thereof;" and that, as we also read, "After this the Lord looked upon the earth, and filled it with His blessings. With all manner of living things hath He covered the face thereof." And if these men are not hopelessly blinded, let them but survey the vast wealth and variety of living creatures, land animals, and winged creatures, and aquatic; and let them understand then that the declaration made by the Lord on the occasion of His judgment of all things is true: "And all things, in accordance with His command, appeared good."

III.—From the Books Against Sabellius. On the Notion that Matter is Ungenerated.

These certainly are not to be deemed pious who hold that matter is ungenerated, while they allow, indeed, that it is brought under the hand of God so far as its arrangement and regulation are concerned; for they do admit that, being naturally passive and pliable, it yields readily to the alterations impressed upon it by God. It is for them, however, to show us plainly how it can possibly be that the like and the unlike should be predicated as subsisting together in God and matter. For it becomes necessary thus to think of one as a superior to either, and that is a thought which cannot legitimately be entertained with regard to God. For if there is this defect of generation which is said to be the thing like in both, and if there is this point of difference which is conceived of besides in the two, whence has this arisen in them? If, indeed, God is the ungenerated, and if this defect of generation is, as we may say, His very essence, then matter cannot be ungenerated; for God and matter are not one and the same. But if each subsists properly and independently—

namely, God and matter—and if the defect of generation also belongs to both, then it is evident that there is something different from each, and older and higher than both. But the difference of their contrasted constitutions is completely subversive of the idea that these can subsist on an equality together, and more, that this one of the two—namely, matter—can subsist of itself. For then they will have to furnish an explanation of the fact that, though both are supposed to be ungenerated, God is nevertheless impassible, immutable, imperturbable, energetic; while matter is the opposite, impressible, mutable, variable, alterable. And now, how can these properties harmoniously co-exist and unite? Is it that God has adapted Himself to the nature of the matter, and thus has skillfully wrought it? But it would be absurd to suppose that God works in gold, as men are wont to do, or hews or polishes stone, or puts His hand to any of the other arts by which different kinds of matter are made capable of receiving form and figure. But if, on the other hand, He has fashioned matter according to His own will, and after the dictates of His own wisdom, impressing upon it the rich and manifold forms produced by His own operation, then is this account of ours one both good and true, and still further one that establishes the position that the ungenerated God is the hypostasis (the life and foundation) of all things in the universe. For with this fact of the defect of generation it conjoins the proper mode of His being. Much, indeed, might be said in confutation of these teachers, but that is not what is before us at present. And if they are put alongside the most impious polytheists, these will seem the more pious in their speech.

IV.—Epistle to Dionysius Bishop of Rome.

From the First Book.

1. There certainly was not a time when God was not the Father.

2. Neither, indeed, as though He had not brought forth these things, did God afterwards beget the Son, but because the Son has existence not from Himself, but from the Father.

And after a few words he says of the Son Himself:—

3. Being the brightness of the eternal Light, He Himself also is absolutely eternal. For since light is always in existence, it is manifest that its brightness also exists, because light is perceived to exist from the fact that it shines, and it is impossible that light should not shine. And let us once more come to illustrations. If the sun exists, there is also day; if nothing of this be manifest, it is impossible that the sun should be there. If then the sun were eternal, the day would never end; but now, for such is not really the state of the case, the day begins with the beginning of the sun, and ends with its ending. But God is the eternal Light, which has neither had a beginning, nor shall ever fail. Therefore the eternal brightness shines forth before Him, and co-exists with Him, in that, existing without a beginning, and always begotten, He always shines before Him; and He is that Wisdom which says, "I was that wherein He delighted, and I was daily His delight before His face at all times."

And a little after he thus pursues his discourse from the same point:—

4. Since, therefore, the Father is eternal, the Son also is eternal, Light of Light. For where there is the begetter, there is also the offspring. And if there is no offspring, how and of what can He be the begetter? But both are, and always are. Since, then, God is the Light, Christ is the Brightness. And since He is a Spirit—for says He, "God is a Spirit"—fittingly again is Christ called Breath; for "He," saith He, "is the breath of God's power."

And again he says:—

5. Moreover, the Son alone, always co-existing with the Father, and filled with Him who is, Himself also is, since He *is* of the Father.

From the Same First Book.

6. But when I spoke of things created, and certain works to be considered, I hastily put forward illustrations of such things, as it were little appropriate, when I said neither is the plant the same as the husbandman, nor the boat the same as the boatbuilder. But then I lingered rather upon things suitable and more adapted to the nature of the thing, and I un- folded in many words, by various carefully considered arguments, what things were more true; which things, moreover, I have set forth to you in another letter. And in these things I have also proved the falsehood of the charge which they bring against me—to wit, that I do not maintain that Christ is consubstantial with God. For although I say that I have never either found or read this word in the sacred Scriptures, yet other reasonings, which I immediately subjoined, are in no wise

discrepant from this view, because I brought forward as an illustration human offspring, which assuredly is of the same kind as the begetter; and I said that parents are absolutely distinguished from their children by the fact alone that they themselves are not their children, or that it would assuredly be a matter of necessity that there would neither be parents nor children. But, as I said before, I have not the letter in my possession, on account of the present condition of affairs; otherwise I would have sent you the very words that I then wrote, yea, and a copy of the whole letter, and I will send it if at any time I shall have the opportunity. I remember, further, that I added many similitudes from things kindred to one another. For I said that the plant, whether it grows up from seed or from a root, is different from that whence it sprouted, although it is absolutely of the same nature; and similarly, that a river flowing from a spring takes another form and name: for that neither is the spring called the river, nor the river the spring, but that these are two things, and that the spring indeed is, as it were, the father, while the river is the water from the spring. But they feign that they do not see these things and the like to them which are written, as if they were blind; but they endeavor to assail me from a distance with expressions too carelessly used, as if they were stones, not observing that on things of which they are ignorant, and which require interpretation to be understood, illustrations that are not only remote, but even contrary, will often throw light.

From the Same First Book.
7. It was said above that God is the spring of all good things, but the Son was called the river flowing from Him; because the word is an emanation of the mind, and—to

speak after human fashion—is emitted from the heart by the mouth. But the mind which springs forth by the tongue is different from the word which exists in the heart. For this latter, after it has emitted the former, remains and is what it was before; but the mind sent forth flies away, and is carried everywhere around, and thus each is in each although one is from the other, and they are one although they are two. And it is thus that the Father and the Son are said to be one, and to be in one another.

From the Second Book.
8. The individual names uttered by me can neither be separated from one another, nor parted. I spoke of the Father, and before I made mention of the Son I already signified

Him in the Father. I added the Son; and the Father, even although I had not previously named Him, had already been absolutely comprehended in the Son. I added the Holy Spirit; but, at the same time, I conveyed under the name whence and by whom He proceeded. But they are ignorant that neither the Father, in that He is *Father*, can be separated from the Son, for that name is the evident ground of coherence and conjunction; nor can the Son be separated from the Father, for this word *Father* indicates association *between* them. And there is, moreover, evident a Spirit who can neither be disjoined from Him who sends, nor from Him who brings Him. How, then, should I who use such names think that these are absolutely divided and separated the one from the other?

After a few words he adds:—
9. Thus, indeed, we expand the indivisible Unity into a Trinity; and again we contract the Trinity, which cannot be diminished, into a Unity.

From the Same Second Book.

10. But if any quibbler, from the fact that I said that God is the Maker and Creator of all things, thinks that I said that He is also Creator of Christ, let him observe that I first called Him Father, in which word the Son also is at the same time expressed. For after I called the Father the Creator, I added, Neither is He the Father of those things whereof He is Creator, if He who begot is properly understood to be a Father (for we will consider the latitude of this word *Father* in what follows). Nor is a maker a father, if it is only a framer who is called a maker. For among the Greeks, they who are wise are said to be makers of their books. The apostle also says, "a doer (*scil.* maker) of the law." Moreover, of matters of the heart, of which kind are virtue and vice, men are called doers (*scil.* makers); after which manner God said, "I expected that it should make judgment, but it made iniquity."

11. That neither must this saying be thus blamed; for he says that he used the name of Maker on account of the flesh which the Word had assumed, and which certainly was made. But if anyone should suspect that that had been said of the Word, even this also was to be heard without contentiousness. For as I do not think that the Word was a thing made, so I do not say that God was its Maker, but its Father. Yet still, if at any time, discoursing of the Son, I may have casually said that God was His Maker, even this mode of speaking would not be without defense. For the wise men among the Greeks call themselves the makers of their books, although the same are fathers of their books. Moreover, divine Scripture calls us makers

of those motions which proceed from the heart, when it calls us doers of the law of judgment and of justice.

From the Same Second Book.
12. *In the beginning was the Word.* But that was not the Word which produced the Word. For "the Word was with God." The Lord is Wisdom; it was not therefore Wisdom that produced Wisdom; for "I was that" says He, "wherein He delighted." Christ is truth; but "blessed," says He, "is the God of truth."

From the Third Book.
13. Life is begotten of life in the same way as the river has flowed forth from the spring, and the brilliant light is ignited from the inextinguishable light

From the Fourth Book.
14. Even as our mind emits from itself a word,—as says the prophet, "My heart hath uttered forth a good word,"—and each of the two is distinct the one from the other, and maintaining a peculiar place, and one that is distinguished from the other; since the former indeed abides and is stirred in the heart, while the latter has its place in the tongue and in the mouth. And yet they are not apart from one another, nor deprived of one another; neither is the mind without the word, nor is the word without the mind; but the mind makes the word and appears in the word, and the word exhibits the mind wherein it was made. And the mind indeed is, as it were, the word immanent, while the word is the mind breaking forth. The mind passes into the word, and the word transmits the mind to the surrounding hearers; and thus the mind by means of the word takes its place in the souls of

the hearers, entering in at the same time as the word. And indeed the mind is, as it were, the father of the word, existing in itself; but the word is as the son of the mind, and cannot be made before it nor without it, but exists with it, whence it has taken its seed and origin. In the same manner, also, the Almighty Father and Universal Mind has before all things the Son, the Word, and the discourse, as the interpreter and messenger of Himself.

About the Middle of the Treatise.
15. If, from the fact that there are three hypostases, they say that they are divided, there are three whether they like it or no, or else let them get rid of the divine Trinity altogether.

And Again:
For on this account after the Unity there is also the most divine Trinity.

The Conclusion of the Entire Treatise.
16. In accordance with all these things, the form, moreover, and rule being received from the elders who have lived before us, we also, with a voice in accordance with them, will both acquit ourselves of thanks to you, and of the letter which we are now writing. And to God the Father, and His Son our Lord Jesus Christ, with the Holy Spirit, be glory and dominion for ever and ever. Amen.

V.—The Epistle to Bishop Basilides.

Canon I.

Dionysius to Basilides, my beloved son, and my brother, a fellow minister with me in holy things, and an obedient servant of God, in the Lord greeting.

You have sent to me, most faithful and accomplished son, in order to inquire what is the proper hour for bringing the fast to a close on the day of Pentecost. For you say that there are some of the brethren who hold that that should be done at cockcrow, and others who hold that it should be at nightfall. For the brethren in Rome, as they say, wait for the cock; whereas, regarding those here, you told us that they would have it earlier. And it is your anxious desire, accordingly, to have the hour presented accurately, and determined with perfect exactness, which indeed is a matter of difficulty and uncertainty. However, it will be acknowledged cordially by all, that from the date of the resurrection of our Lord, those who up to that time have been humbling their souls with fastings, ought at once to begin their festal joy and gladness. But in what you have written to me you have made out very clearly, and with an intelligent understanding of the Holy Scriptures, that no very exact account seems to be offered in them of the hour at which He rose. For the evangelists have given different descriptions of the parties who came to the sepulcher one after another, and all have declared that they found the Lord risen already. It was "in the end of the Sabbath," as Matthew has said; it was "early, when it was yet dark," as John writes; it was "very early in the morning," as Luke puts it; and it was "very early in the morning, at the rising of the sun," as Mark tells us. Thus no one has shown us clearly the exact time when He rose. It is admitted, however, that those who came to the sepulcher in the end of the Sabbath, as it began to dawn toward the first day of the week, found Him no longer lying in it. And let us not suppose that the evangelists disagree or contradict each other. But even although there may seem to be some small difficulty as to the subject of our inquiry, if they all agree that the light of the world, our Lord, rose on that one night, while they differ with respect to the hour, we may well seek with wise and faithful mind to harmonize their statements. The narrative by Matthew then, runs thus: "In the end of the Sabbath as it began to dawn toward the first day of the week, came Mary Magdalene, and the other Mary, to see the sepulcher. And, behold, there was a great earthquake: for the angel of the Lord descended from heaven, and came and rolled back the stone, and sat upon it. And his countenance was like lightning, and his raiment white as snow: and for fear of him the keepers did shake, and became as dead men. And the angel answered and said unto the women, Fear not ye: for I know that ye seek Jesus, which was crucified. He is not here; for He is risen, as He said." Now this phrase "in the end" will be thought by some to signify, according to the common use of the word, the *evening* of the Sabbath; while others, with a better perception of the fact, will say that it does not indicate that, but *a late hour in the night*, as the phrase "in the end" denotes slowness and length of time. Also because he speaks of *night*, and not of *evening*, he has added the words, "as it began to dawn toward the first day of the week." And the parties here did not come yet, as the others say, "bearing spices," but "to see the sepulcher;" and they discovered the occurrence of the earthquake, and the angel sitting upon the stone, and heard from him the declaration, "He is not here, He is risen." And to the same effect is the testimony of John. "The first day of the week," says he, "came Mary Magdalene early, when it was yet dark, unto the sepulcher, and sees the stone taken away from the sepulcher." Only, according to this "when it was yet dark," she had come in advance. And Luke says: "They rested the Sabbath-day, according to the commandment. Now, upon the first day of the week, very early in the morning, they came unto the sepulcher, bringing the spices which they had prepared; and they found the stone rolled away from the sepulcher." This phrase "very early in the morning" probably indicates the early dawn of the first day of the week; and thus, when the Sabbath itself was wholly past, and also the whole night succeeding it, and when another day had begun, they came, bringing spices and myrrh, and then it became apparent that He had already risen long before. And Mark follows this, and says: "They had bought sweet spices, in order that they might come and anoint Him. And very early (in the morning), the first day of the week, they come unto the sepulcher at the rising of the sun." For this evangelist also has used the term "very early," which is just the same as the "very early in the morning" employed by the former; and he has added, "at the rising of the sun." Thus they set out, and took their way first when it was "very early in the morning," or (as Mark says) when it was "very early;" but on the road, and by their stay at the sepulcher, they spent the time till it was sunrise. And then the young man clad in white said to them, "He is risen, He is not here." As the case stands thus, we make the following statement and explanation to those who seek an exact account of the specific hour, or half-hour, or quarter of an hour, at which it is proper to begin their rejoicing over our Lord's rising from the dead. Those who are too hasty, and give up even before midnight, we reprehend as remiss and intemperate, and as almost breaking off from their course in their precipitation, for it is a wise man's word, "That is not little in life which is within a little." And those who hold out and continue for a very long time, and persevere even on to the fourth watch, which is also the time at which our Savior manifested Himself walking upon the sea to those who were then on the deep, we receive as noble and laborious disciples. On those, again, who pause and refresh themselves in the course as they are moved or as they are able, let us not press very hard: for all do not carry out the six days of fasting either equally or alike; but some pass even all the days as a fast, remaining without food through the whole; while others take but two, and others three, and others four, and others not even one. And to those who have labored painfully through these protracted fasts. and have thereafter become exhausted and well-nigh undone, pardon ought to be extended if they are somewhat precipitate in taking food. But if there are any who not only decline such protracted fasting, but refuse at the first to fast at all, and rather indulge themselves luxuriously during the first four days, and then when they reach the last two days—viz., the preparation and the Sabbath—fast with due rigor during these, and these alone, and think that they do something grand and brilliant if they hold out till the morning, I cannot think that they have gone through the time on equal terms with those who have been practicing the same during several days before. This is the counsel which, in accordance with my apprehension of the question, I have offered you in writing on these matters.

Canon II.

The question touching women in the time of their separation, whether it is proper for them when in such a condition to enter the house of God, I consider a superfluous inquiry. For I do not think that, if they are believing and pious women, they will themselves be rash enough in such a condition either to approach the holy table or to touch the body and blood of the Lord. Certainly the woman who had the issue of blood of twelve years' standing did not touch *the Lord* Himself, but only the hem of His garment, with a view to her cure. For to pray, however a person may be situated, and to remember the Lord, in whatever condition a person may be, and to offer up petitions for the obtaining of help, are exercises altogether blameless. But the individual who is not perfectly pure both in soul and in body, shall be interdicted from approaching the holy of holies.

Canon III.

Moreover, those who are competent, and who are advanced in years, ought to be judges of themselves in these matters. For that it is proper to abstain from each other by consent, in order that they may be free for a season to give themselves to prayer, and then come together again, they have heard from Paul in his epistle.

Canon IV.

As to those who are overtaken by an involuntary flux in the night-time, let such follow the testimony of their own conscience, and consider themselves as to whether they are doubtfully minded in this matter or not. And he that doubted in the matter of meats, the apostle tells us, "is damned if he eat." In these things, therefore, let everyone who approaches God be of a good conscience, and of a proper confidence, so far as his own judgment is concerned. And, indeed, it is in order to show your regard for us (for you are not ignorant, beloved,) that you have proposed these questions to us, making us of one mind, as indeed we are, and of one spirit with yourself. And I, for my part, have thus set forth my opinions in public, not as a teacher, but only as it becomes us with all simplicity to confer with each other. And when you have examined this opinion of mine, my most intelligent son, you will write back to me your notion of these matters, and let me know whatever may seem to you to be just and preferable, and whether you approve of my judgment in these things. That it may fare well with you, my beloved son, as you minister to the Lord in peace, is my prayer.

Part II.—Containing Epistles, or Fragments of Epistles.

Epistle I.—To Domitius and Didymus.

1. But it would be a superfluous task for me to mention by name our (martyr) friends, who are numerous and at the same time unknown to you. Only understand that they include men and women, both young men and old, both maidens and aged matrons, both soldiers and private citizens,— every class and every age, of whom some have suffered by

stripes and fire, and some by the sword, and have won the victory and received their crowns. In the case of others, however, even a very long lifetime has not proved sufficient to secure their appearance as men acceptable to the Lord; as indeed in my own case too, that sufficient time has not shown itself up to the present. Wherefore He has preserved me for another convenient season, of which He knows Himself, as He says: "In an acceptable time have I heard thee, and in a day of salvation have I helped thee."

2. Since, however, you have been inquiring about what has befallen us, and wish to be informed as to how we have fared, you have got a full report of our fortunes; how when we—that is to say, Gaius, and myself, and Faustus, and Peter, and Paul—were led off as prisoners by the centurion and the magistrates, accompanying them, there came upon us certain parties from Mareotis, who dragged us with them against our will, and though we were disinclined to follow them, and carried us away by force; and how Gaius and Peter and myself have been separated from our other brethren, and shut up alone in a desert and sterile place in Libya, at a distance of three days' journey from Parætonium.

3. *And a little further on, he proceeds thus*:—And they concealed themselves in the city, and secretly visited the brethren. I refer to the presbyters Maximus, Dioscorus, Demetrius, and Lucius. For Faustinus and Aquila, who are persons of greater prominence in the world, are wandering about in Egypt. I specify also the deacons who survived those who died in the sickness, viz., Faustus, Eusebius, and Chæremon. And of Eusebius I speak as one whom the Lord strengthened from the beginning, and qualified for the task of discharging energetically the services due to the confessors who are in prison, and of executing the perilous office of dressing out and burying the bodies of

those perfected and blessed martyrs. For even up to the present day the governor does not cease to put to death, in a cruel manner, as I have already said, some of those who are brought before him; while he wears others out by torture, and wastes others away with imprisonment and bonds, commanding also that no one shall approach them and making strict scrutiny lest anyone should be seen to do so. And nevertheless God imparts relief to the oppressed by the tender kindness and earnestness of the brethren.

Epistle II.—To Novatus

Dionysius to Novatus his brother, greeting. If you were carried on against your will, as you say, you will show that such has been the case by your voluntary retirement. For it would have been but dutiful to have suffered any kind of ill, so as to avoid rending the Church of God. And a martyrdom borne for the sake of preventing a division of the Church, would not have been more inglorious than one endured for refusing to worship idols; nay, in my opinion at least, the former would have been a nobler thing than the latter. For in the one case a person gives such a testimony simply for his own individual soul, whereas in the other case he is a witness for the whole Church. And now, if you can persuade or constrain the brethren to come to be of one mind again, your uprightness will be superior to your error; and the latter will not be charged against you, while the former will be com- mended in you. But if you cannot prevail so far with your recusant brethren, see to it that you save your own soul. My wish is, that in the Lord you may fare well as you study peace.

Epistle III.—To Fabius, Bishop of Antioch.

1. The persecution with us did not commence with the imperial edict, but preceded it by a whole year. And a certain prophet and poet, an enemy to this city, whatever else he was, had previously roused and exasperated against us the masses of the heathen, inflaming them anew with the fires of their native superstition. Excited by him, and finding full liberty for the perpetration of wickedness, they reckoned this the only piety *and* service to their demons, namely, our slaughter.

2. First, then, they seized an old man of the name of Metras, and commanded him to utter words of impiety; and as he refused, they beat his body with clubs, and lacerated his face and eyes with sharp reeds, and then dragged him off to the suburbs and stoned him there. Next they carried off a woman named Quinta, who was a believer, to an idol temple, and compelled her to worship the idol; and when she turned away from it, and showed how she detested it, they bound her feet and dragged her through the whole city along the rough stone-paved streets, knocking her at the same time against the millstones, and scourging her, until they brought her to the same place, and stoned her also there. Then with one im- pulse they all rushed upon the houses of the God-fearing, and whatever pious persons any of them knew individually as neighbors, after these they hurried and bore them with them, and robbed and plundered them, setting aside the more valuable portions of their property for themselves, and scattering about the commoner articles, and such as were made of wood, and burning them on the roads, so that they made these parts present the spectacle of a city taken by the enemy. The

brethren, however, simply gave way and withdrew, and, like those to whom Paul bears witness, they took the spoiling of their goods with joy. And I know not that any of them—except possibly some solitary individual who may have chanced to fall into their hands—thus far has denied the Lord.

3. But they also seized that most admirable virgin Apollonia, then in advanced life, and knocked out all her teeth, and cut her jaws; and then kindling a fire before the city, they threatened to burn her alive unless she would repeat along with them their expressions of impiety. And although she seemed to deprecate her fate for a little, on being let go, she leaped eagerly into the fire and was consumed. They also laid hold of a certain Serapion in his own house; and after torturing him with severe cruelties, and breaking all his limbs, they dashed him headlong from an upper story to the ground. And there was no road, no thoroughfare, no lane even, where we could walk, whether by night or by day; for at all times and in every place they all kept crying out, that if anyone should refuse to repeat their blasphemous expressions, he must be at once dragged off and burnt. These inflictions were carried rigorously on for a considerable time in this manner. But when the insurrection and the civil war in due time overtook these wretched people, that diverted their savage cruelty from us, and turned it against themselves. And we enjoyed a little breathing time, as long as leisure failed them for exercising their fury against us.

4. But speedily was the change from that kindlier reign announced to us; and great was the terror of threatening that was now made to reach us. Already, indeed, the edict had arrived; and it was of such a tenor as almost perfectly to correspond with what was intimated to us before time by our Lord, setting before us the most

dreadful horrors, so as, if that were possible, to cause the very elect to stumble. All verily were greatly alarmed, and of the more notable there were some, and these a large number, who speedily accommodated themselves to the decree in fear; others, who were engaged in the public service, were drawn into compliance by the very necessities of their official duties; others were dragged on to it by their friends, and on being called by name approached the impure and unholy sacrifices; others yielded pale and trembling, as if they were not to offer sacrifice, but to be themselves the sacrifices and victims for the idols, so that they were jeered by the large multitude surrounding the scene, and made it plain to all that they were too cowardly either to face death or to offer the sacrifices. But there were others who hurried up to the altars with greater alacrity, stoutly asserting that they had never been Christians at all before; of whom our Lord's prophetic declaration holds most true, that it will be hard for such to be saved. Of the rest, some followed one or other of these parties *already mentioned*; some fled, and some were seized. And of these, some went as far *in keeping their faith* as bonds and imprisonment; and certain persons among them endured imprisonment even for several days, and then after all abjured the faith before coming into the court of justice; while others, after holding out against the torture for a time, sank before the prospect of further sufferings.

5. But there were also others, steadfast and blessed pillars of the Lord, who, receiving strength from Himself, and obtaining power and vigor worthy of and commensurate with the force of the faith that was in themselves, have proved admirable witnesses for His kingdom. And of these the first was Julianus, a man

suffering from gout, and able neither to stand nor to walk, who was arranged along with two other men who carried him. Of these two persons, the one immediately denied *Christ*; but the other, a person named Cronion, and surnamed Eunus, and together with him the aged Julianus himself, confessed the Lord, and were carried on camels through the whole city, which is, as you know, a very large one, and were scourged in that elevated position, and finally were consumed in a tremendous fire, while the whole populace surrounded them. And a certain soldier who stood by them when they were led away to execution, and who opposed the wanton insolence of the people, was pursued by the outcries they raised against him; and this most courageous soldier of God, Besas by name, was arranged; and after bearing himself most nobly in that mighty conflict on behalf of piety, he was beheaded. And another individual, who was by birth a Libyan, and who at once in name and in real blessedness was also a true Macar, although much was tried by the judge to persuade him to make a denial, did not yield, and was consequently burned alive. And these were succeeded by Epimachus and Alexander, who, after a long time spent in chains, and after suffering countless agonies and inflictions of the scraper and the scourge, were also burnt to ashes in an immense fire.

6. And along with these there were four women. Among them was Ammonarium, a pious virgin, who was tortured for a very long time by the judge in a most relentless manner, because she declared plainly from the first that she would utter none of the things which he commanded her to repeat; and after she had made good her profession she was led off to execution. The others were the most venerable and aged Mercuria, and

Dionysia, who had been the mother of many children, and yet did not love her offspring better than her Lord.

These, when the governor was ashamed to subject them any further to profitless torments, and thus to see himself beaten by women, died by the sword, without more experience of tortures. For truly their champion Ammonarium had received tortures for them all.

7. Heron also, and Ater, and Isidorus who were Egyptians, and along with them Dioscorus, a boy of about fifteen years of age, were delivered up. And though at first he, *the judge,* tried to deceive the youth with fair speeches, thinking he could easily seduce him, and then attempted also to compel him by force of tortures, fancying he might be made to yield without much difficulty in that way, Dioscorus neither submitted to his persuasions nor gave way to his terrors. And the rest, after their bodies had been lacerated in a most savage manner, and their steadfastness had nevertheless been maintained, he consigned also to the flames. But Dioscorus he dismissed, wondering at the distinguished appearance he had made in public, and at the extreme wisdom of the answers he gave to his interrogations, and declaring that, on account of his age, he granted him further time for repentance. And this most godly Dioscorus is with us at present, tarrying for a greater conflict and a more lengthened contest. A certain person of the name of Nemesion, too, who was also an Egyptian, was falsely accused of being a companion of robbers; and after he had cleared himself of this charge before the centurion, and proved it to be a most unnatural calumny, he was in- formed against as a Christian, and had to come as a prisoner before the governor. And that most unrighteous magistrate inflicted on him a punishment

Dionysius

twice as severe as that to which the robbers were subjected, making him suffer both tortures and scourgings, and then consigning him to the fire between the robbers. Thus the blessed martyr was honored after the pattern of Christ.

8. There was also a body of soldiers, including Ammon, and Zeno, and Ptolemy, and Ingenuus, and along with them an old man, Theophilus, who had taken up their position in a mass in front of the tribunal; and when a certain person was standing his trial as a Christian, and was already inclining to make a denial, these stood round about and ground their teeth, and made signs with their faces, and stretched out their hands, and made all manner of gestures with their bodies. And while the attention of all was directed to them, before any could lay hold of them, they ran quickly up to the bench of judgment and declared themselves to be Christians, and made such an impression that the governor and his associates were filled with fear; and those who were under trial seemed to be most courageous in the prospect of what they were to suffer, while the judges themselves trembled. These, then, went with a high spirit from the tribunals, and exulted in their testimony, God Himself causing them to triumph gloriously.

9. Moreover, others in large numbers were torn asunder by the heathen throughout the cities and villages. Of one of these I shall give some account, as an example. Ischyrion served one of the rulers in the capacity of steward for stated wages. His employer ordered this man to offer sacrifice; and on his refusal to do so, he abused him. When he persisted in his non- compliance, his master treated him with contumely; and when he still held out, he took a huge stick and thrust it through his bowels and heart, and

slew him. Why should I mention the multitudes of those who had to wander about in desert places and upon the mountains, and who were cut off by hunger, and thirst, and cold, and sickness, and robbers, and wild beasts? The survivors of such are the witnesses of their election and their victory. One circumstance, however, I shall subjoin as an illustration of these things. There was a certain very aged person of the name of Chæremon, bishop of the place called the city of the Nile. He fled along with his partner to the Arabian mountain, and never returned. The brethren, too, were unable to discover anything of them, although they made frequent search; and they never could find either the men themselves, or their bodies. Many were also carried off as slaves by the barbarous Saracens to that same Arabian mount. Some of these were ransomed with difficulty, and only by paying a great sum of money; others of them have not been ransomed to this day. And these facts I have related, brother, not without a purpose, but in order that you may know how many and how terrible are the ills that have befallen us; which troubles also will be best understood by those who have had most experience of them.

10. Those sainted martyrs, accordingly, who were once with us, and who now are seated with Christ, and are sharers in His kingdom, and partakers with Him in His judgment and who act as His judicial assessors, received there certain of the brethren who had fallen away, and who had become chargeable with sacrificing to the idols. And as they saw that the conversion and repentance of such might be acceptable to Him who desires not at all the death of the sinner, but rather his repentance, they proved their sincerity, and received them, and brought them together again, and assembled with them,

Dionysius

and had fellowship with them in their prayers and at their festivals. What advice then, brethren, do you give us as regards these? What should we do? Are we to stand forth and act with the decision and judgment which those (martyrs) formed, and to observe the same graciousness with them, and to deal so kindly with those toward whom they showed such compassion? or are we to treat their decision as an unrighteous one, and to constitute ourselves judges of their opinion on such subjects, and to throw clemency into tears, and to overturn the established order?

11. But I shall give a more particular account of one case here which occurred among us: There was with us a certain Serapion, an aged believer. He had spent his long life blamelessly, but had fallen in the time of trial (the persecution). Often did this man pray (for absolution), and no one gave heed to him; sick, he continued three successive days dumb and senseless. Recovering a little on the fourth day, he called to him his grandchild, and said, "My son, how long do you detain me? Hasten, I entreat you, and absolve me quickly. Summon one of the presbyters to me." And when he had said this, he became speechless again. The boy ran for the presbyter; but it was night, and the man was sick, and was consequently unable to come. But as an injunction had been issued by me, that persons at the point of death, if they requested it then, and especially if they had earnestly sought it before, should be absolved, in order that they might depart this life in cheerful hope, he gave the boy a small portion of the Eucharist, telling him to steep it in water and drop it into the old man's mouth. The boy returned bearing the portion; and as he came near, and before he had yet entered, Serapion again recovered, and said, "You have

come, my child, and the presbyter was unable to come; but do quickly what you were instructed to do, and so let me depart." The boy steeped the morsel in water, and at once dropped it into the (old man's) mouth; and after he had swallowed a little of it, he forthwith gave up the ghost. Was he not then manifestly preserved? and did he not continue in life just until he could be absolved, and until through the wiping away of his sins he could be acknowledged for the many good acts he had done?

Epistle IV.—To Cornelius the Roman Bishop
_____

In addition to all these, he writes likewise to Cornelius at Rome after receiving his Epistle against Novatus. And in that letter he also shows that he had been invited by Helenus, bishop in Tarsus of Cilicia, and by the others who were with him—namely, Firmilian, bishop in Cappadocia, and Theoctistus in Palestine—to meet them at the Council of Antioch, where certain persons were attempting to establish the schism of Novatus. In addition to this, he writes that it was reported to him that Fabius was dead, and that Demetrianus was appointed his successor in the bishopric of the church at Antioch. He writes also respecting the bishop in Jerusalem, expressing himself in these very words: "And the blessed Alexander, having been cast into prison, went to his rest in blessedness."

Epistle V.—Which is the First on the Subject of Baptism Addressed to Stephen, Bishop of Rome.
_____

Understand, however, my brother, that all the churches located in the east, and also in remoter districts, that were formerly in a state of division, are now made one again; and all those at the head of the churches everywhere are of one mind, and rejoice exceedingly at the peace which has been restored beyond all expectation. I may mention Demetrianus in Antioch; Theoctistus in Cæsareia; Mazabanes in Ælia, the successor of the deceased Alexander; Marinus in Tyre; Heliodorus in Laodicea, the successor of the deceased Thelymidres; Helenus in Tarsus, and with him all the churches of Cilicia; and Firmilian and all Cappadocia. For I have named only the more illustrious of the bishops, so as neither to make my epistle too long, nor to render my discourse too heavy for you. All the districts of Syria, however, and of Arabia, to the brethren in which you from time to time have been forwarding supplies and at present have sent letters, and Mesopotamia too, and Pontus, and Syria, and, to speak in brief, all parties, are everywhere rejoicing at the unanimity and brotherly love now established, and are glorifying God for the same.

The Same, Otherwise Rendered.

But know, my brother, that all the churches throughout the East, and those that are placed beyond, which formerly were separated, are now at length returned to unity; and all the presidents *of the churches* everywhere think one and the same thing, and rejoice with incredible joy on account of the unlooked-for return of peace: to wit, Demetrianus in Antioch; Theoctistus in Cæsarea; Mazabenes in Ælia, after the death of Alexander; Marinus in Tyre; Heliodorus in Laodicea, after the death of Thelymidres; Helenus in Tarsus, and all the churches of Cilicia; Firmilianus, with all Cappadocia. And I have named only the more illustrious bishops, lest by chance my letter should be made too prolix, and my address too wearisome. The whole of the Syrias, indeed, and Arabia, to which you now and then send help, and to which you have now written letters; Mesopotamia also, and Pontus, and Bithynia; and, to comprise all in one word, all the lands everywhere, are rejoicing, praising God on account of this concord and brotherly charity.

Epistle VI.—To Sixtus, Bishop

1. Previously, indeed, (Stephen) had written letters about Helanus and Firmilianus, and about all who were established throughout Cilicia and Cappadocia, and all the neighboring provinces, giving them to understand that for that same reason he would depart from their communion, because they rebaptized heretics. And consider the seriousness of the matter. For, indeed, in the most considerable councils of the bishops, as I hear, it has been decreed that they who come from heresy should first be trained in *Catholic* doctrine, and then should be cleansed by baptism from the filth of the old and impure leaven. Asking and calling him to witness all these matters, I sent letters.

And a little after Dionysius proceeds:—

2. And, moreover, to our beloved co-presbyters Dionysius and Philemon, who before agreed with Stephen, and had written to me about the same matters, I wrote previously in few words, but now I have written again more at length.

In the same letter, says Eusebius, he informs Xystus of the Sabellian heretics, that they were gaining ground at that time, in these words:—

3. For since of the doctrine, which lately has been set on foot at Ptolemais, a city of Pentapolis, impious and full of blasphemy against Almighty God and the Father of our Lord Jesus Christ; full of unbelief and perfidy towards His only begotten Son and the first-born of every creature, the Word made man, and which takes away the perception of the Holy Spirit,—on either side both letters were brought to me, and brethren had come to discuss it, setting forth more plainly as much as by God's gift I was able,—I wrote certain letters, copies of which I have sent to thee.

Epistle VII.—To Philemon, a Presbyter.

I indeed gave attention to reading the books and carefully studying the traditions of heretics, to the extent indeed of corrupting my soul with their execrable opinions; yet receiving from them this advantage, that I could refute them in my own mind, and detested them more heartily than ever. And when a certain brother of the order of presbyters sought to deter me, and feared lest I should be involved in the same wicked filthiness, because he said that my mind would be contaminated, and indeed with truth, as I myself perceived, I was strengthened by a vision that was sent me from God. And a word spoken to me, expressly commanded me, saying, Read everything which shall come into thy hands, for thou art fit to do so, who corrects and proves each one; and from them to thee first of all has appeared the cause and the occasion of believing. I received this vision as being what was in accordance with the apostolic word, which thus urges all who are endowed with greater virtue, "Be ye skillful money-changers."

Then, says Eusebius, he subjoins some things parenthetically about all heresies:—

This rule and form I have received from our blessed Father Heraclus: For thou, who came from heresies, even if they had fallen away from the Church, much rather if they had not fallen away, but when they were seen to frequent the assemblies of the faithful, were charged with going to hear the teachers of perverse doctrine, and ejected from the Church, he did not admit after many prayers, before they had openly and publicly narrated whatever things they had heard from their adversaries. Then he received them at length to the assemblies of the faithful, by no means asking of them to receive baptism anew. Because they had already previously received the Holy Spirit from that very baptism.

Once more, this question being thoroughly ventilated, he adds:—

I learned this besides, that this custom is not now first of all imported among the Africans alone; but moreover, long before, in the times of former bishops, among most populous churches, and that when synods of the brethren of Iconium and Synades were held, it also pleased as many as possible, I should be unwilling, by overturning their judgments, to throw them into strife and contentious. For it is written, "Thou shalt not remove thy neighbor's landmark, which thy fathers have placed."

Epistle VIII.—To Dionysius

For we rightly repulse Novatian, who has rent the Church, and has drawn away some of the brethren to impiety and blasphemies; who has brought into the world a most impious doctrine concerning God, and calumniates our most merciful Lord Jesus Christ as if He were unmerciful; and besides all these things, holds the sacred laver as of no effect, and rejects it, and overturns faith and confession, which are put before baptism, and utterly drives away the Holy Spirit from them, even if any hope subsists either that He would abide in them, or that He should return to them.

Epistle IX.—To Sixtus II

For truly, brother, I have need of advice, and I crave your judgment, lest perchance I should be mistaken upon the matters which in such wise happen to me. One of the brethren who come together to the church, who for some time has been esteemed as a believer, and who before my ordination, and, if I am not deceived, before even the episcopate of Heraclas himself, had been a partaker of the assembly of the faithful, when he had been concerned in the baptism of those who were lately baptized, and had heard the interrogatories and their answers, came to me in tears, and bewailing his lot. And throwing himself at my feet, he began to confess and to protest that this baptism by which he had been initiated among heretics was not of this kind, nor had it anything whatever in common with this of ours, because that it was full of blasphemy and impiety. And he said that his soul was pierced with a very bitter sense of sorrow, and that he did not dare even to lift up his eyes to God, because he had been initiated by those wicked words and things. Wherefore he besought that, by this purest laver, he might be endowed with adoption and grace. And I, indeed, have not dared to do this; but I have said that the long course of communion had been sufficient for this. For I should not dare to renew afresh, after all, one who had heard the giving of thanks, and who had answered with others Amen; who had stood at the holy table, and had stretched forth his hands to receive the blessed food, and had received it, and for a very long time had been a partaker of the body and blood of our Lord Jesus Christ. Henceforth I bade him be of good courage, and approach to the sacred *elements* with a firm faith and a good conscience, and become a partaker of them. But he makes no end of his wailing, and shrinks from approaching the table; and scarcely, when entreated, can he bear to be present at the prayers.

Epistle X.—Against Bishop Germanus

1. Now I speak also before God, and He knows that I lie not: it was not by my own choice, neither was it without divine instruction, that I took to flight. But at an earlier period, indeed, when the *edict for the* persecution under Decius was determined upon, Sabinus at that very hour sent a certain Frumentarius to make search for me. And I remained in the house for four days, expecting the arrival of this Frumentarius. But he went about examining

all other places, the roads, the rivers, the fields, where he suspected that I should either conceal myself or travel. And he was smitten with a kind of blindness, and never lighted on the house; for he never supposed that I should tarry at home when under pursuit. Then, barely after the lapse of four days, God giving me instruction to remove, and opening the way for me in a manner beyond all expectation, my domestics and I, and a considerable number of the brethren, effected an exit together. And that this was brought about by the providence of God, was made plain by what followed: in which also we have been perhaps of some service to certain parties.

2. *Then, after a certain break, he narrates the events which befell him after his flight, subjoining the following statement*:—Now about sunset I was seized, along with those who were with me, by the soldiers, and was carried off to Taposiris. But by the providence of God, it happened that Timotheus was not present with me then, nor indeed had he been apprehended at all. Reaching the place later, he found the house deserted, and officials keeping guard over it, and ourselves borne into slavery.

3. *And after some other matters, he proceeds thus*:— And what was the method of this marvelous disposition of Providence in his case? For the real facts shall be related. When Timotheus was fleeing in great perturbation, he was met by a man from the country. This person asked the reason for his haste, and he told him the truth plainly. Then the man (he was on his way at the time to take part in certain marriage festivities; for it is their custom to spend the whole night in such gatherings), on hearing the fact, held on his course to the scene of the rejoicings, and went in and narrated the circumstances to those who were seated at the feast; and with a single impulse, as if it had been at a

given watchword, they all started up, and came on all in a rush, and with the utmost speed. Hurrying up to us, they raised a shout; and as the soldiers who were guarding us took at once to flight, they came upon us, stretched as we were upon the bare couches. For my part, as God knows, I took them at first to be robbers who had come to plunder and pillage us; and remaining on the bedstead on which I was lying naked, save only that I had on my linen underclothing, I offered them the rest of my dress as it lay beside me. But they bade me get up and take my departure as quickly as I could. Then I understood the purpose of their coming, and cried, entreated, and implored them to go away and leave us alone; and I begged that, if they wished to do us any good, they might anticipate those who led me captive, and strike off my head. And while I was uttering such vociferations, as those who were my comrades and partners in all these things know, they began to lift me up by force. And I threw myself down on my back upon the ground; but they seized me by the hands and feet, and dragged me away, and bore me forth. And those who were witnesses of all these things followed me,—namely, Caius, Faustus, Peter, and Paul. These men also took me up, and hurried me off out of the little town, and set me on an ass without saddle, and in that fashion carried me away.

4. I fear that I run the risk of being charged with great folly and senselessness, placed as I am under the necessity of giving a narrative of the wonderful dispensation of God's providence in our case. Since, however, as one says, it is good to keep close the secret of a king, but it is honorable to reveal the works of God, I shall come to close quarters with the violence of Germanus. I came to Æmilianus not alone; for there

accompanied me also my co-presbyter Maximus, and the deacons Faustus and Eusebius and Chæremon; and one of the brethren who had come from Rome went also with us. Æmilianus, then, did not lead off by saying to me, "Hold no assemblies." That was indeed a thing superfluous for him to do, and the last thing which one would do who meant to go back to what was first and of prime importance: for his concern was not about our gathering others together in assembly, but about our not being Christians ourselves. From this, therefore, he commanded me to desist, thinking, doubtless, that if I myself should recant, the others would also follow me in that. But I answered him neither unreasonably nor in many words, "We must obey God rather than men." Moreover, I testified openly that I worshipped the only true God and none other, and that I could neither alter that position nor ever cease to be a Christian. Thereupon he ordered us to go away to a village near the desert, called Cephro.

5. Hear also the words which were uttered by both of us as they have been put on record. When Dionysius, and Faustus, and Maximus, and Marcellus, and Chæremon had been placed at the bar, Æmilianus, as prefect, said: "I have reasoned with you verily in free speech, on the clemency of our sovereigns, as they have suffered you to experience it; for they have given you power to save yourselves, if you are disposed to turn to what is accordant with nature, and to worship the gods who also maintain them in their kingdom, and to forget those things which are repugnant to nature. What say ye then to these things? for I by no means expect that you will be ungrateful to them for their clemency, since indeed what they aim at is to bring you over to better courses." Dionysius made reply thus: "All men do not worship all the gods, but

different men worship different objects that they sup- pose to be true gods. Now we worship the one God, who is the Creator of all things, and the very Deity who has committed the sovereignty to the hands of their most sacred majesties Valerian and Gallienus. Him we both reverence and worship; and to Him we pray continually on behalf of the sovereignty of these princes, that it may abide unshaken." Æmilianus, as prefect, said to them: "But who hinders you from worshipping this god too, if indeed he is a god, along with those who are gods by nature? for you have been commanded to worship the gods, and those gods whom all know as such." Dionysius replied: "We worship no other one." Æmilianus, as prefect, said to them: "I perceive that you are at once ungrateful to and insensible of the clemency of our princes. Wherefore you shall not remain in this city; but you shall be dispatched to the parts of Libya, and settled in a place called Cephro: for of this place I have made choice in accordance with the command of our princes. It shall not in any wise be lawful for you or for any others, either to hold assemblies or to enter those places which are called cemeteries. And if anyone is seen not to have betaken himself to this place whither I have ordered him to repair, or if he be discovered in any assembly, he will prepare peril for himself; for the requisite punishment will not fail. Be off, therefore, to the place whither you have been commanded to go." So he forced me away, sick as I was; nor did he grant me the delay even of a single day. What opportunity, then, had I to think either of holding assemblies, or of not holding them?

6. *Then after some other matters he says*:—Moreover, we did not withdraw from the visible assembling of ourselves together, with the Lord's presence. But those in

the city I tried to gather together with all the greater zeal, as if I were present with them; for I was absent indeed in the body, as I said, but present in the spirit. And in Cephro indeed a considerable church sojourned with us, composed partly of the brethren who followed us from the city, and partly of those who joined us from Egypt. There, too, did God open to us a door for the word. And at first we were persecuted, we were stoned; but after a period some few of the heathen forsook their idols, and turned to God. For by our means the word was then sown among them for the first time, and before that they had never received it. And as if to show that this had been the very purpose of God in conducting us to them, when we had fulfilled this ministry, He led us away again. For Æmilianus was minded to remove us to rougher parts, as it seemed, and to more Libyan-like districts; and he gave orders to draw all in every direction into the Mareotic territory, and assigned villages to each party throughout the country. But he issued instructions that we should be located specially by the public way, so that we might also be the first to be apprehended; for he evidently made his arrangements and plans with a view to an easy seizure of all of us whenever he should make up his mind to lay hold of us.

7. Now when I received the command to depart to Cephro, I had no idea of the situation of the place, and had scarcely even heard its name before; yet for all that, I went away courageously and calmly. But when word was brought me that I had to remove to the parts of Colluthion, those present know how I was affected; for here I shall be my own accuser. At first, indeed, I was greatly vexed, and took very ill; for though these places happened to be better known and more familiar to us, yet

people declared that the region was one destitute of brethren, and even of men of character, and one exposed to the annoyances of travelers and to the raids of robbers. I found comfort, however when the brethren reminded me that it was nearer the city; and while Cephro brought us large intercourse with brethren of all sorts who came from Egypt, so that we were able to hold our sacred assemblies on a more extensive scale, yet there, on the other hand, as the city was in the nearer vicinity, we could enjoy more frequently the sight of those who were the really beloved, and in closest relation- ship with us, and dearest to us: for these would come and take their rest among us, and, as in the more remote suburbs, there would be distinct and special meetings. And thus it turned out.

8. *Then, after some other matters, he gives again the following account of what befell him:*

—Germanus, indeed, boasts himself of many professions of faith. He, forsooth, is able to speak of many adverse things which have happened to him! Can he then reckon up in his own case as many condemnatory sentences as we can number in ours, and confiscations too, and proscriptions, and spoiling of goods, and losses of dignities, worldly honor, and contemnings of the laudations of governors and councilors, and patient subjections to the threatening of the adversaries, and to outcries, and perils, and persecutions, and a wandering life, and the pressure of difficulties, and all kinds of trouble, such as befell me in the time of Decius and Sabinus, and such also as I have been suffering under the present severities of Æmilianus? But where in the world did Germanus make his appearance? And what mention is made of him? But I retire from this huge act of folly into which I am suffering myself to fall on account of Germanus; and accordingly I forbear giving to the brethren, who already have full knowledge of these things, a particular and detailed narrative of all that happened.

Epistle XI.—To Hermammon

1. But Gallus did not understand the wickedness of Decius, nor did he note beforehand what it was that wrought his ruin. But he stumbled at the very stone which was lying before his eyes; for when his sovereignty was in a prosperous position, and when affairs were turning out according to his wish, he oppressed those holy men who interceded with God on behalf of his peace and his welfare. And consequently, persecuting them, he persecuted also the prayers offered in his own behalf.

2. And to John a revelation is made in like manner: "And there was given unto him," he says, "a mouth speaking great things, and blasphemy; and power was given unto him, and forty and two months." And one finds both things to wonder at in Valerian's case; and most especially has one to consider how different it was with him before these events,—how mild and well-disposed he was towards the men of God. For among the emperors who preceded him, there was not one who exhibited so kindly and favorable a disposition toward them as he did; yea, even those who were said to have become Christians openly did not receive them with that extreme friendliness and graciousness with which he received them at the beginning of his reign; and his whole house was filled then with the pious, and it was itself a very church of God. But the master and president of the Magi of Egypt prevailed on him to abandon that course,

urging him to slay and persecute those pure and holy men as adversaries and obstacles to their accursed and abominable incantations. For there are, indeed, and there were men who, by their simple presence, and by merely showing themselves, and by simply breathing and uttering some words, have been able to dissipate the artifices of wicked demons. But he put it into his mind to practice the impure rites of initiation, and detestable juggleries, and execrable sacrifices, and to slay miserable children, and to make oblations of the offspring of unhappy fathers, and to divide the bowels of the newly-born, and to mutilate and cut up the creatures made by God, as if by such means they would attain to blessedness.

3. *Afterwards he subjoins the following*:—Splendid surely were the thank-offerings, then, which Macrianus brought them for that empire which was the object of his hopes; who, while formerly reputed as the sovereign's faithful public treasurer, had yet no mind for anything which was either reasonable in itself or conducive to the public good, but subjected himself to that curse of prophecy which says, "Woe unto those who prophesy from their own heart, and see not the public good!" For he did not discern that providence which regulates all things; nor did he think of the judgment of Him who is before all, and through all, and over all. Wherefore he also became an enemy to His Catholic Church; and besides that, he alienated and estranged himself from the mercy of God, and fled to the utmost possible distance from His salvation. And in this indeed he demonstrated the reality of the peculiar significance of his name.

4. *And again, after some other matters, he proceeds thus*:—For Valerian was instigated to these acts by this man, and was thereby exposed to contumely and

reproach, according to the word spoken *by the Lord* to Isaiah: "Yea, they have chosen their own ways, and their own abominations in which their souls delighted; I also will choose their mockeries, and will recompense their sin." But this man (Macrianus), being maddened with his passion for the empire, all unworthy of it as he was, and at the same time having no capacity for assuming the insignia of imperial government, by reason of his crippled body, put forward his two sons as the bearers, so to speak, of their father's offences. For unmistakably apparent in their case was the truth of that declaration made by God, when He said, "Visiting the iniquities of the fathers upon the children, unto the third and fourth generation of them that hate me." For he heaped his own wicked passions, for which he had failed in securing satisfaction, upon the heads of his sons, and thus wiped off upon them his own wickedness, and transferred to them, too, the hatred he himself had shown toward God.

5. That man, then, after he had betrayed the one and made war upon the other of the emperors preceding him, speedily perished, with his whole family, root and branch. And Gallienus was proclaimed, and acknowledged by all. And he was at once an old emperor and a new; for he was prior to those, and he also survived them. To this effect indeed is the word spoken *by the Lord* to Isaiah: "Behold, the things which were from the beginning have come to pass; and there are new things which shall now arise." For as a cloud which intercepts the sun's rays, and overshadows it for a little, obscures it, and appears itself in its place, but again, when the cloud has passed by or melted away, the sun, which had risen before, comes forth again and shows itself: so did this Macrianus put himself forward, and achieve access for himself even to

the very empire of Gallienus now established; but now he is *that* no more, because indeed he never was it, while this other, *i.e., Gallienus*, is just as he was. And his empire, as if it had cast off old age, and had purged itself of the wickedness formerly attaching to it, is at present in a more vigorous and flourishing condition, and is now seen and heard of at greater distances, and stretches abroad in every direction.

6. *Then he further indicates the exact time at which he wrote this account, as follows*:—And it occurs to me again to review the days of the imperial years. For I see that those most impious men, whose names may have been once so famous, have in a short space become nameless. But our more pious and godlier prince has passed his septennium, and is now in his ninth year, in which we are to celebrate the festival.

Epistle XII.—To the Alexandrians

1. To other men, indeed, the present state of matters would not appear to offer a fit season for a festival: and this certainly is no festal time to them; nor, in sooth, is any other that to them. And I say this, not only of occasions manifestly sorrowful, but even or all occasions whatsoever which people might consider to be most joyous. And now certainly all things are turned to mourning, and all men are in grief, and lamentations resound through the city, by reason of the multitude of the dead and of those who are dying day by day. For as it is written in the case of the first-born of the Egyptians, so now too a great cry has arisen. "For there is not a house in

which there is not one dead." And would that even this were all!

2. Many terrible calamities, it is true, have also befallen us before this. For first they drove us away; and though we were quite alone, and pursued by all, and in the way of being slain, we kept our festival, even at such a time. And every place that had been the scene of some of the successive sufferings which befell any of us, became a seat for our solemn assemblies,—the field, the desert, the ship, the inn, the prison,—all alike. The most gladsome festival of all, however, has been celebrated by those perfect martyrs who have sat down at the feast in heaven. And after these things war and famine surprised us. These were calamities which we shared, indeed, with the heathen. But we had also to bear by ourselves alone those ills with which they outraged us, and we had at the same time to sustain our part in those things which they either did to each other or suffered at each other's hands; while again we rejoiced deeply in that peace of Christ which He imparted to us alone.

3. And after we and they together had enjoyed a very brief season of rest, this pestilence next assailed us,—a calamity truly more dreadful to them than all other objects of dread, and more intolerable than any other kind of trouble whatsoever; and a misfortune which, as a certain writer of their own declares, alone prevails over all hope. To us, however, it was not so; but in no less measure than other ills it proved an instrument for our training and probation. For it by no means kept aloof from us, although it spread with greatest violence among the heathen.

4. *To these statements he in due succession makes this addition*:—Certainly very many of our brethren, while, in their exceeding love and brotherly-kindness, they did not spare themselves, but kept by each other, and visited the sick without thought of their own peril, and ministered to them assiduously, and treated them for their healing in Christ, died from time to time most joyfully along with them, lading themselves with pains derived from others, and drawing upon themselves their neighbors' diseases, and willingly taking over to their own persons the burden of the sufferings of those around them. had thus cured others of their sicknesses, and restored them to strength, died themselves, having transferred to their own bodies the death that lay upon these. And that common saying, which else seemed always to be only a polite form of address, they expressed in actual fact then, as they departed this life, like the "*off-scourings of all*." Yea, the very best of our brethren have departed this life in this manner, including some presbyters and some deacons, and among the people those who were in highest reputation: so that this very form of death, in virtue of the distinguished piety and the steadfast faith which were exhibited in it, appeared to come in nothing beneath martyrdom itself.

5. And they took the bodies of the saints on their upturned hands, and on their bosoms, and closed their eyes, and shut their mouths. And carrying them in company, and laying them out decently, they clung to them, and embraced them, and prepared them duly with washing and with attire. And then in a little while after they had the same services done for themselves, as those who survived were ever following those who departed before them. But among the heathen all was the very reverse. For they thrust aside any who began to be sick, and kept aloof even from their dearest friends, and cast the sufferers out upon the public roads half dead, and left them unburied, and treated them with utter contempt when they died, steadily avoiding any kind of communication and intercourse with death; which, however, it was not easy for them altogether to escape, in spite of the many precautions they employed.

Epistle XIII.—To Hierax, a Bishop in Egypt.

1. But what wonder should there be if I find it difficult to communicate by letter with those who are settled in remote districts, when it seems beyond my power even to reason with myself, and to take counsel with my own soul? For surely epistolary communications are very requisite for me with those who are, as it were, my own bowels, my closest associates, and my brethren—one in soul with myself, and members, too, of the same Church. And yet no way opens up by which I can transmit such addresses. Easier, indeed, would it be for one, I do not say merely to pass beyond the limits of the province, but to cross from east to west, than to travel from this same Alexandria to Alexandria. For the most central pathway in this city is vaster and more impassable even than that extensive and untrodden desert which Israel only traversed in two generations; and our smooth and waveless harbors have become an image of that sea through which the people drove, at the time when it divided itself and stood up like walls on either side, and in whose thoroughfare the Egyptians were drowned. For often they have appeared like the Red Sea, inconsequence of the slaughter perpetrated in them. The river, too, which flows by the city, has sometimes appeared drier than the waterless

desert, and more parched than that wilderness in which Israel was so overcome with thirst on their journey, that they kept crying out against Moses, and the water was made to stream for them from the precipitous rock by the power of Him who alone doeth wondrous things. And sometimes, again, it has risen in such flood-tide, that it has overflowed all the country round about, and the roads, and the fields, as if it threatened to bring upon us once more that deluge of waters which occurred in the days of Noah.

2. But now it always flows onward, polluted with blood and slaughters and the drowning struggles of men, just as it did of old, when on Pharaoh's account it was changed by Moses into blood, and made putrid. And what other liquid could cleanse water, which itself cleanses all things? How could that ocean, so vast and impassable for men, though poured out on it, ever purge this bitter sea? Or how could even that great river which streams forth from Eden, though it were to discharge the four hearts into which it is divided into the one channel of the Gihon, wash away these pollutions? Or when will this air, befouled as it is by noxious exhalations which rise in every direction, become pure again? For there are such vapors sent forth from the earth, and such blasts from the sea, and breezes from the rivers, and reeking mists from the harbors, that for dew we might suppose ourselves to have the impure fluids of the corpses which are rotting in all the underlying elements. And yet, after all this, men are amazed, and are at a loss to understand whence come these constant pestilences, whence these terrible diseases, whence these many kinds of fatal inflictions, whence all that large and multiform destruction of human life, and what reason there is why this mighty city no longer contains within it as great a number of inhabitants, taking all parties into account,

from tender children up to those far advanced in old age, as once it maintained of those alone whom it called hale old men. But those from forty years of age up to seventy were so much more numerous then, that their number cannot be made up now even when those from fourteen to eighty years of age have been added to the roll and register of persons who are recipients of the public allowances of grain. And those who are youngest in appearance have now become, as it were, equals in age with those who of old were the most aged. And yet, although they thus see the human race constantly diminishing and wasting away upon the earth, they have no trepidation in the midst of this increasing and advancing consumption and annihilation of their own number.

Epistle XIV.—From His Fourth Festival Epistle

Love is altogether and forever on the alert, and casts about to do some good even to one who is unwilling to receive it. And many a time the man who shrinks from it under a feeling of shame, and who declines to accept services of kindness on the ground of unwillingness to become troublesome to others, and who chooses rather to bear the burden of his own grievances than cause annoyance and anxiety to any one, is importuned by the man who is full of love to bear with his aids, and to suffer himself to be helped by another, though it might be as one sustaining a wrong, and thus to do a very great service, not to himself, but to another, in permitting that other to be the agent in putting an end to the ill in which he has been involved.

Elucidations.

(Apocalypse, note 7, p. 105, and note 9, p. 106.)

The moderation of Dionysius is hardly less conspicuous than his fearlessness of inquiry in the questions he raises about the Apocalypse. He utterly refuses to reject it. He testifies to the value set upon it by his fellow-Christians. Only, he doubts as to (*the* John) the "inspired person" who was its author, and with critical skill exposes the inferiority of the Greek of the Apocalypse to that of the Gospel and Epistles of St. John. Obviously he accepts it as part of the canon, only doubting as to the author. Modestly he owns that it passes his understanding. So Calvin forbore to comment upon it, and owned to "headache" when he came to it.

Exegetical Fragments.

I.—A Commentary on the Beginning of Ecclesiastes.

Chapter I.

Ver. 1. "*The words* of the son of David, king of Israel in Jerusalem." In like manner also Matthew calls the Lord the son of David.

3. "What profit hath a man of all his labor which he taketh under the sun?"

For what man is there who, although he may have become rich by toiling after the objects of this earth, has been able to make himself three cubits in stature, if he is naturally only of two cubits in stature? Or who, if blind, has by these means recovered his sight? Therefore we ought to direct our toils to a goal beyond the sun: for thither, too, do the exertions of the virtues reach.

4. "One generation passes away, and another generation comes: but the earth abides forever" (unto the age).

Yes, unto the age, but not unto the ages.

16. "I communed with mine own heart, saying, Lo, I am come to great estate, and have gotten more wisdom than all they that have been before me in Jerusalem; yea, my heart had great experience of wisdom and knowledge.

17. I knew parables and science: that this indeed is also the spirit's choice

18. For in multitude of wisdom is multitude of knowledge: and he that increases knowledge increases grief."

I was vainly puffed up, and increased wisdom; not the wisdom which God has given, but that wisdom of which Paul says, "The wisdom of this world is foolishness with God."

For in this Solomon had also an experience surpassing prudence, and above the measure of all the ancients. Consequently he shows the vanity of it, as what follows in like manner demonstrates: "And my heart uttered many things: I knew wisdom, and knowledge, and parables, and sciences." But this was not the genuine wisdom or knowledge, but that which, as Paul says, puffed up. He spoke, moreover, as it is written, three thousand parables. But these were not parables of a spiritual kind, but only such as fit the common polity of men; as, for instance, utterances about animals or medicines. For which reason he has added in a tone of raillery, "I knew that this also is the spirit's choice." He speaks also of the multitude of knowledge, not the knowledge of the Holy Spirit, but that which the prince of this world works, and which he conveys to men in order to overreach their souls, with officious questions as to the measures of heaven, the position of earth, the bounds of the sea. But he says also, "He that increases knowledge increases sorrow." For they search even into things deeper than these,—inquiring, for example, what necessity there is for fire to go upward, and for water to go downward; and when they have learned that it is because the one is light and the other heavy, they do but increase sorrow: for the question still remains, Why might it not be the very reverse?

Chapter II.

Ver. 1. "I said in mine heart, Go to now, make trial as in mirth, and behold in good.

And this, too, is vanity."

For it was for the sake of trial, and in accordance with what comes by the loftier and the severe life, that he entered into pleasure. And he makes mention of the mirth, which men call so. And he says, "in good," referring to what men call good things, which are not capable of giving life to their possessor, and which make the man who engages in them vain like themselves.

2. "I said of laughter, It is mad; and of mirth, What does thou?"

Laughter has a twofold madness; because madness begets laughter, and does not allow the sorrowing for sins; and also because a man of that sort is possessed with madness, in the confusing of seasons, and places, and persons. For he flees from those who sorrow. "And to mirth, What does thou?" Why dost thou repair to those who are not at liberty to be merry? Why to the drunken, and the avaricious, and the rapacious? And why this phrase, "as wine?" Because wine makes the heart merry; and it acts upon the poor in spirit. The flesh, however, also makes the heart merry, when it acts in a regular and moderate fashion.

3. "And my heart directed me in wisdom, and to overcome in mirth, until I should know what is that good thing to the sons of men which they shall do under the sun for the number of the days of their life."

Being directed, he says, by wisdom, I overcame pleasures in mirth. Moreover, for me the aim of knowledge was to occupy myself with nothing vain, but to find the good; for if a person finds that, he does not miss the discernment also of the profitable. The sufficient is also the opportune, and is commensurate with the length of life.

4. "I made me great works; I built me houses; I planted me vineyards.

5. I made me gardens and orchards.

6. I made me pools of water, that by these I might rear woods producing trees.

7. I got me servants and maidens, and had servants born in my house; also I had large possessions of great and small cattle above all that were in Jerusalem before me.

8. I gathered me also silver and gold, and the peculiar treasure of kings and of the provinces. I got me men-singers and women-singers, and the delights of the sons of men, as cups and the cupbearer.

9. And I was great, and increased more than all that were before me in Jerusalem: also my wisdom remained with me.

10. And whatsoever mine eyes desired, I kept not from them; I withheld not my heart from any pleasure."

You see how he reckons up a multitude of houses and fields, and the other things which he mentions, and then finds nothing profitable in them. For neither was he any better in soul by reason of these things, nor by their means did he gain friendship with God. Necessarily he is led to speak also of the true riches and the abiding property. Being minded, therefore, to show what kinds of possessions remain with the possessor, and continue steadily and maintain themselves for him, he adds: "Also my wisdom remained with me." For this alone remains, and all these other things, which he has already reckoned up, flee away and depart. Wisdom, therefore, remained with me, and I remained in virtue of it. For those other things fall, and also cause the fall of the very persons who run after them. But, with the intention of instituting a comparison between wisdom and those things which are held to be good among men, he adds these words, "And whatsoever mine eyes desired, I kept not from them," and so forth; whereby he describes as evil, not only those toils which they endure who toil in gratifying themselves with pleasures, but those, too, which by necessity and constraint men have to sustain for their maintenance day by day, laboring at their different occupations in the sweat of their faces. For the labor, he says, is great; but the art by the labor is temporary, adding nothing serviceable among things that please. Wherefore there is no profit. For where there is no excellence there is no profit. With reason, therefore, are the objects of such solicitude but vanity, and the spirit's choice. Now this name of "spirit" he gives to the "soul." For choice is a quality, not a motion. And David says: "Into Thy hands I commit my spirit." And in good truth "did my wisdom remain with me," for it made me know and understand, so as to enable me to speak of all that is not advantageous under the sun. If, therefore, we desire the righteously profitable, if we seek the truly advantageous, if it is our aim to be incorruptible, let us engage those labors which reach beyond the sun. For in these there is no vanity, and there is not the choice of a spirit at once inane and hurried hither and thither to no purpose.

12. "And I turned myself to behold wisdom, and madness, and folly: for what man is there that shall come after counsel in all those things which it has done?"

He means the wisdom which comes from God, and which also remained with him. And by madness and folly he designates all the labors of men, and the vain and silly pleasure they have in them. Distinguishing these, therefore, and their measure, and blessing the true wisdom, he has added: "For what man is there that shall come after counsel?" For this counsel instructs us in the wisdom that is such indeed, and gifts us with deliverance from madness and folly.

13. "Then I saw that wisdom exceled folly, as much as light exceled darkness."

He does not say this in the way of comparison. For things which are contrary to each other, and mutually destructive, cannot be compared. But his decision was, that the one is to be chosen, and the other avoided. To like effect is the saying, "Men loved darkness rather than light." For the term "rather" in that passage expresses the choice of the person loving, and not the comparison of the objects themselves.

14. "The wise man's eyes are in his head, but the fool walketh in darkness."

That man always inclines earthward, he means, and has the ruling faculty darkened. It is true, indeed, that we men have all of us our eyes in our head, if we speak of the mere disposition of the body. But he speaks here of the eyes of the mind. For as the eyes of the swine do not turn naturally up towards heaven, just because it is made by nature to have an inclination toward the belly; so the mind of the man who has once been enervated by pleasures is not easily diverted from the tendency thus assumed, because he has not "respect unto all the commandments of the Lord." Again: "Christ is the head of the Church."

And they, therefore, are the wise who walk in His way; for He Himself has said, "I am the way." On this account, then, it becomes the wise man always to keep the eyes of his mind directed toward Christ Himself, in order that he may do nothing out of measure, neither being lifted up in heart in the time of prosperity, nor becoming negligent in the day of adversity: "for His judgments are a great deep," as you will learn more exactly from what is to follow.

14."And I perceived myself also that one event happened to them all.

15,Then said I in my heart, As it happened to the fool, so it happened even to me; and why was I then more wise?"

The run of the discourse in what follows deals with those who are of a mean spirit as regards this present life, and in whose judgment the article of death and all the anomalous pains of the body are a kind of dreaded evil, and who on this account hold that there is no profit in a life of virtue, because there is no difference made in ills like these between the wise man and the fool. He speaks consequently of these as the words of a madness inclining to utter senselessness; whence he also adds this sentence,

"For the fool talks over-much;" and by the "fool" here he means himself, and everyone who reasons in that way. Accordingly he condemns this absurd way of thinking. And for the same reason he has given utterance to such sentiments in the fears of his heart; and dreading the righteous condemnation of those who are to be heard, he solves the difficulty in its pressure by his own reflections. For this word, "Why was I then wise?" was the word of a man in doubt and difficulty whether what is expended on wisdom is done well or to no purpose; and whether there is no difference between the wise man and the fool in point of advantage, seeing that the former is involved equally with the latter in the same sufferings which happen in this present world. And for this reason he says, "I spoke over-largely in my heart," in thinking that there is no difference between the wise man and the fool.

16. "For there is no remembrance of the wise equally with the fool forever."

For the events that happen in this life are all transitory, be they even the painful incidents, of which he says, "As all things now are consigned to oblivion." For after a short space has passed by, all the things that befall men in this life perish in forgetfulness. Yea, the very persons to whom these things have happened are not remembered all in like manner, even although they may have gone through like chances in life. For they are not remembered for these, but only for what they may have evinced of wisdom or folly, virtue or vice. The memories of such are not extinguished (equally) among men in consequence of the changes of lot befalling them. Wherefore he has added this: "And how shall the wise man die along with the fool? The death of sinners, indeed, is evil: yet the memory of the just is blessed, but the name of the wicked is extinguished."

22. "For that falls to man in all his labor."

In truth, to those who occupy their minds with the distractions of life, life becomes a painful thing, which, as it were, wounds the heart with its goads, that is, with the lustful desires of increase. And sorrowful also is the solicitude connected with covetousness: it does not so much gratify those who are successful in it, as it pains those who are unsuccessful; while the day is spent in laborious anxieties, and the night puts sleep to flight from the eyes, with the cares of making gain. Vain, therefore, is the zeal of the man who looks to these things.

24. And there is nothing good for a man, but what he eats and drinks, and what will show to his soul good in his labor. This also I saw, that it is from the hand of God.

25. For who eats and drinks from his own resources?" That the discourse does not deal now with material meats, he will show by what follows; namely, "It is better to go to the house of mourning than to go to the house of feasting." And so in the present passage he proceeds to add: "And (what) will show to his soul good in its labor." And surely mere material meats and drinks are not the soul's good. For the flesh, when luxuriously nurtured, wars against the soul, and rises in revolt against the spirit. And how should not intemperate eating and drinking also be contrary to God? He speaks, therefore, of things mystical. For no one shall partake of the spiritual table, but one who is called by Him, and who has listened to the wisdom which says, "Take and eat."

Chapter III.

Ver. 3. "There is a time to kill, and a time to heal."

To "kill," in the case of him who perpetrates unpardonable transgression; and to "heal," in the case of him who can show a wound that will bear remedy.

4. "A time to weep, and a time to laugh."

A time to weep, when it is the time of suffering; as when the Lord also says, "Verily I say unto you, that ye shall weep and lament." But to laugh, as concerns the resurrection: "For your sorrow," He says, "shall be turned into joy."

4. "A time to mourn, and a time to dance."

When one thinks of the death which the transgression of Adam brought on us, it is a time to mourn; but it is a time to hold festal gatherings when we call to mind the resurrection from the dead which we expect through the new Adam.

6. "A time to keep, and a time to cast away."

A time to keep the Scripture against the unworthy, and a time to put it forth for the worthy. Or, again: Before the incarnation it was a time to keep the letter of the law; but it was a time to cast it away when the truth came in its flower.

7. "A time to keep silence, and a time to speak."

A time to speak, when there are hearers who receive the word; but a time to keep silence, when the hearers pervert the word; as Paul says: "A man that is a heretic, after the first and second admonition, reject."

10. "I have seen, then, the travail which God hath given to the sons of men to be exercised in it.

11. Everything that He hath made is beautiful in its time: and He hath set the whole world in their heart; so that no man can find out the work that God maketh from the beginning and to the end."

And this is true. For no one is able to comprehend the works of God altogether. Moreover, the world is the work of God. No one, then, can find out as to this world what is its space from the beginning and unto the end, that is to say, the period appointed for it, and the limits before determined unto it; forasmuch as God has set the whole world as *a realm of* ignorance in our hearts. And thus one says: "Declare to me the shortness of my days." In this manner, and for our profit, the end of this world (age)—that is to say, this present life—is a thing of which we are ignorant.

II.—The Gospel According to Luke. An Interpretation.—Chap. XXII. 42–48

Ver. 42. "Father, if Thou be willing to remove this cup from me: nevertheless not my will, but Thine, be done."

But let these things be enough to say on the subject of the will. This word, however, "Let the cup pass," does not mean, Let it not come near me, or approach me. For what can "pass from Him," certainly must first come nigh Him; and what does pass thus from Him, must be by Him. For if it does not reach Him, it cannot pass from Him. For He takes to Himself the person of man, as having been made man. Wherefore also on this occasion He deprecates the doing of the inferior, which is His own, and begs that the superior should be done, which is His Father's, to wit, the divine will; which again, however, in respect of the divinity, is one and the same will in Himself and in the Father. For it was the Father's will that He should pass through every trial (temptation); and the Father Himself in a marvelous manner brought Him on this course, not indeed with the trial itself as His goal, nor in order simply that He might enter into that, but in order that He might prove Himself to be above the trial, and also beyond it. And surely it is the fact, that the Savior asks neither what is impossible, nor what is impracticable, nor what is contrary to the will of the Father. It is something possible; for Mark makes mention of His saying, "Abba, Father, all things are possible unto Thee." And they are possible if He wills them; for Luke tells us that He said, "Father, if Thou be willing, remove this cup from me." The Holy Spirit, therefore, apportioned among the evangelists, makes up the full account of our Savior's whole disposition by the expressions of these several narrators together. He does not, then, ask of the Father what the Father wills not. For the words, "If Thou be willing," were demonstrative of subjection and docility, not of ignorance or hesitancy. For this reason, the other scripture says, "All things are possible unto Thee." And Matthew again admirably describes the submission and humility when he says, "If it be possible." For unless I adapt the sense in this way, some will perhaps assign an impious signification to this expression, "If it be possible;" as if there were anything impossible for God to do, except that only which He does not will to do. But...being straightway strengthened in His humanity by His ancestral divinity, he urges the safer petition, and desires no longer that should be the case, but that it might be accomplished in accordance with the Father's good pleasure, in glory, in constancy, and in fulness. For John, who has given us the record of the sublimest and divinest of the Savior's words and deeds, heard Him speak thus: "And the cup which my Father hath given me, shall I not drink it?" Now, to drink the cup was to discharge the ministry and the whole economy of trial with fortitude, to follow and fulfill the Father's determination, and to surmount all apprehensions. And the exclamation, "Why hast Thou forsaken me?" was in due accordance with the requests He had previously made: Why is it that death has been in conjunction with me all along up till now, and that I bear not yet the cup? This I judge to have been the Savior's meaning in this concise utterance.

And He certainly spoke truth then. Nevertheless He was not forsaken. But He drank out the cup at once, as His plea had implied, and then passed away. And the vinegar which was handed to Him seems to me to have been a symbolic thing. For the turned wine indicated very well the quick turning and change which He sustained, when He passed from His passion to impassibility, and from death to deathlessness, and from the position of one judged to that of one judging, and from subjection under the despot's power to the exercise of kingly dominion. And the sponge, as I think, signified the complete transfusion of the Holy Spirit that was realized in Him. And the reed symbolized the royal scepter and the divine law. And the hyssop expressed that quickening and saving resurrection of His, by which He has also brought health to us.

43. "And there appeared an angel unto Him from heaven, strengthening Him.

44. And being in an agony, He prayed more earnestly; and His sweat was as it were great drops of blood falling down to the ground."

The phrase, "a sweat of blood," is a current parabolic expression used of persons in intense pain and distress; as also of one in bitter grief people say that the man "weeps tears of blood." For in using the expression, "as it were great drops of blood," he does not declare the drops of sweat to have been actually drops of blood. For he would not then have said that these drops of sweat were like blood. For such is the force of the expression, "as it were great drops." But rather with the object of making it plain that the Lord's body was not be- dewed with any kind of subtle moisture which had only the show and appearance of actuality, but that it was really suffused all over with sweat in the shape of large thick drops, he has taken the great drops of blood as an illustration of what was the case with Him. And accordingly, as by the intensity of the supplication and the severe agony, so also by the dense and excessive sweat, he made the facts patent, that the Savior was man by nature and in reality, and not in mere semblance and appearance, and that He was subject to all the innocent sensibilities natural to men. Nevertheless the words, "I have power to lay down my life, and I have power to take it again," show that His passion was a voluntary thing; and besides that, they indicate that the life which is laid down and taken again is one thing, and the divinity which lays that down and takes it again is another.

He says, "one thing and another," not as making a partition into two persons, but as showing the distinction between the two natures.

And as, by voluntarily enduring the death in the flesh, He implanted incorruptibility in it; so also, by taking to Himself of His own free-will the passion of our servitude, He set in it the seeds of constancy and courage, whereby He has nerved those who believe on Him for the mighty conflicts belonging to their witness-bearing. Thus, also, those drops of sweat flowed from Him in a marvelous way like great drops of blood, in order that He might, as it were, drain off and empty the fountain of the fear which is proper to our nature. For unless this had been done with a mystical import, He certainly would not, even had He been the most timorous and ignoble of men, have been bedewed in this unnatural way with drops of sweat like drops of blood under the mere force of His agony.

Of like import is also the sentence in the narrative which tells us that an angel stood by the Savior and strengthened Him. For this, too, bore also on the economy entered into on our behalf. For those who are appointed to engage in the sacred exertions of conflicts on account of piety, have the angels from heaven to assist them. And the prayer, "Father, remove the cup," He uttered probably not as if He feared the death itself, but with the view of challenging the devil by these words to erect the cross for Him. With words of deceit that personality deluded Adam; with the words of divinity, then, let the deceiver himself now be deluded. How be it assuredly the will of the Son is not one thing, and the will of the Father another. For He who wills what the Father wills, is found to have the Father's will. It is in a figure, therefore, that He says, "not my will, but Thine." For it is not that He wishes the cup to be removed, but that He refers to the Father's will the right issue of His passion, and honors thereby the Father as the First. For if the fathers style one's disposition *gnomè*, and if such disposition relates also to what is in consideration hidden as if by settled purpose, how say some that the Lord, who is above all these things, bears a gnomic will? Manifestly that can be only by defect of reason.

45. "And when He rose from prayer, and was come to His disciples, He found them sleeping for sorrow;

46. And said unto them, Why sleep ye? Rise and pray, lest ye enter into temptation."

For in the most general sense it holds good that it is apparently not possible for any man to remain altogether without experience of ill. For, as one says, the whole world lieth in wickedness;" and again, "The most of the days of man are labor and trouble." But you will perhaps say, What difference is there between being tempted, and falling or entering into temptation? Well, if one is overcome of evil—and he will be overcome unless he struggles against it himself, and unless God protects him with His shield—that man has entered into temptation, and is in it, and is brought under it like one that is led captive. But if one with- stands and endures, that man is indeed tempted; but he has not entered into temptation, or fallen into it. Thus Jesus was led up of the Spirit, not indeed to enter into temptation, but to be tempted of the devil. And Abraham, again, did not enter into temptation, neither did God lead him into temptation, but He tempted (tried) him; yet He did not drive him into temptation. The Lord Himself, moreover, tempted (tried) the disciples. Thus the wicked one, when he tempts us, draws us into the temptations, as dealing himself with the temptations of evil. But God, when He tempts (tries), adduces the temptations (trials) as one untempted of evil. For God, it is said, "cannot be tempted of evil." The devil, therefore, drives us on by violence, drawing us to destruction; but God leads us by hand, training us for our salvation.

47."And while He yet spoke, behold a multitude, and he that was called Judas, one of the twelve, went before them, and drew near unto Jesus, and kissed Him.

48. But Jesus said unto him, Judas, betrays thou the Son of man with a kiss?

How wonderful this endurance of evil by the Lord, who even kissed the traitor, and spoke words softer even than the kiss! For He did not say, O thou abominable, yea, utterly abominable traitor, is this the return you make to us for so great kindness? But, somehow, He says simply "Judas," using the proper name, which was the address that would be used by one who commiserated a person, or who wished to call him back, rather than of one in anger. And He did not say, "thy Master, the Lord, thy benefactor;" but He said simply, "the Son of man," that is, the tender and meek one: as if He meant to say, Even supposing that I was not your Master, or Lord, or benefactor, dost thou still betray one so guilelessly and so tenderly affected towards thee, as even to kiss thee in the hour of thy treachery, and that, too, when the kiss was the signal for thy treachery? Blessed art Thou, O Lord! How great is this example of the endurance of evil that Thou hast shown us in Thine own person! how great, too, the pattern of lowliness! Howbeit, the Lord has given us this example, to show us that we ought not to give up offering our good counsel to our brethren, even should nothing remarkable be affected by our words.

For as incurable wounds are wounds which cannot be remedied either by severe applications, or by those which may act more pleasantly upon them; so the soul, when it is once carried captive, and gives itself up to any kind of wickedness, and refuses to consider what is really profitable for it, although a myriad counsels should echo in it, takes no good to itself. But just as if the sense of hearing were dead within it, it receives no benefit from exhortations addressed to it; not because it cannot, but only because it will not. This was what happened in the case of Judas. And yet Christ, although He knew all these things beforehand, did not at any time, from the beginning on to the end, omit to do all in the way of counsel that depended on Him. And inasmuch as we know that such was His practice, we ought also unceasingly to endeavor to set those right who prove careless, even although no actual good may seem to be effected by that counsel.

III.—On Luke XXII. 42, Etc.

But let these things be enough to say on the subject of the will. This word, however, "Let the cup pass," does not mean, Let it not come near me, or approach me. For what can pass from Him must certainly first come nigh Him, and what does thus pass from Him must be by Him. For if it does not reach Him, it cannot pass from Him. Accordingly, as if He now felt it to be present, He began to be in pain, and to be troubled, and to be sore amazed, and to be in an agony. And as if it was at hand and placed before Him, He does not merely say "the cup," but He indicates it by the word "this." Therefore, as what passes from one is something which neither has no approach nor is permanently settled with one, so the Savior's first request is that the temptation which has come softly and plainly upon Him, and associated itself lightly with Him, may be turned aside. And this is the first form of that freedom from falling into temptation, which He also counsels the weaker disciples to make the subject of their prayers; that, namely, which concerns the approach of temptation: for it must needs be that offences come, but yet those to whom they come ought not to fall into the temptation. But the most perfect mode in which this freedom from entering into temptation is exhibited, is what He expresses in His second request, when He says not merely, "Not as I will," but also, "but as Thou wilt."

For with God there is no temptation in evil; but He wills to give us good exceeding abundantly above what we ask or think. That His will, therefore, is the perfect will, the Beloved Himself knew; and often does He say that He has come to do that will, and not His own will,—that is to say, the will of men. For He takes to Himself the person of men, as having been made man. Wherefore also on this occasion He deprecates the doing of the inferior, which is His own, and begs that the superior should be done, which is His Father's, to wit, the divine will, which again, however, in respect of the divinity, is one and the same will in Himself and in His Father. For it was the Father's will that He should pass through every trial (temptation), and the Father Himself in a marvelous manner brought Him on this course; not indeed, with the trial itself as His goal, nor in order simply that He might enter into that, but in order that He might prove Himself to be above the trial, and also beyond it. And surely it is the fact that the Savior asks neither what is impossible, nor what is impracticable, nor what is contrary to the will of the Father. It is something possible, for Mark makes mention of His saying, "Abba, Father, all things are possible unto Thee;" and they are possible if He wills them, for Luke tells us that He said, "Father, if Thou be willing, remove this cup from me." The Holy Spirit therefore, apportioned among the evangelists, makes up the full account of our Savior's whole disposition by the expressions of these several narrators together. He does not then ask of the Father what the Father wills not. For the words, "if Thou be willing," were demonstrative of subjection and docility, not of ignorance or hesitancy. And just as when we make any request that may be accordant with his judgment, at the hand of father or ruler or any one of those whom we respect, we are accustomed to use the address, though not certainly as if we were in doubt about it, "if you please;" so the Savior also said, "if Thou be willing:" not that He thought that He willed something different, and thereafter learned the fact, but that He understood exactly God's willingness to remove the cup from Him, and as doing so also apprehended justly that what He wills is also possible unto Him. For this reason the other scripture says, "All things are possible unto Thee." And Matthew again admirably describes the submission and the humility, when he says, "if it be possible." For unless we adapt the sense in this way, some will perhaps assign an impious signification to this expression "if it be possible," as if there were anything impossible for God to do, except that only which He does not will to do. Therefore the request which He made was nothing independent, nor one which pleased Himself only, or opposed His Father's will, but one also in conformity with the mind of God. And yet someone may say that He is overborne and changes His mind, and asks presently something different from what He asked before, and holds no longer by His own will, but introduces His Father's will. Well, such truly is the case. Nevertheless He does not by any means make any change from one side to another; but He embraces another way, and a different method of carrying out one and the same transaction, which is also a thing agreeable to both; choosing, to wit, in place of the mode which is the inferior, and which appears unsatisfying also to Himself, the superior and more admirable mode marked out by the Father. For no doubt He did pray that the cup might pass from Him; but He says also, "Nevertheless, not as I will, but as Thou wilt." He longs painfully, on the one hand, for its passing from Him, but (He knows that) it is better as the Father wills. For He does not utter a petition for its not passing away now, instead of one for its removal; but when its withdrawal is now before His view, He chooses rather that this should be ordered as the Father wills. For there is a twofold kind of withdrawal: there is one in the instance of an object that has shown itself and reached another, and is gone at once on being followed by it or on outrunning it, as is the case with racers when they graze each other in passing; and there is another in the instance of an object that has sojourned and tarried with another, and sat down by it, as in the case of a marauding band or a camp, and that after a time withdraws on being conquered, and on gaining the opposite of a success. For if they prevail they do not retire, but carry off with them those whom they have reduced; but if they prove unable to win the mastery, they withdraw themselves in disgrace. Now it was after the former similitude that He wished that the cup might come into His hands, and promptly pass from Him again very readily and quickly; but as soon as He spoke thus, being at once strengthened in His humanity by the Father's divinity, He urges the safer petition, and desires no longer that that should be the case, but that it might be accomplished in accordance with the Father's good pleasure, in glory, in constancy, and in fulness. For John, who has given us the record of the sublimest and divinest of the Savior's words and deeds, heard Him speak thus: "And the cup which my Father hath given me, shall I not drink it?" Now, to drink the cup was to discharge the ministry and the whole economy of trial with fortitude, to follow and fulfil the Father's determination, and to surmount all apprehensions; and, indeed, in the very prayer which He uttered He showed that He was leaving these (apprehensions) behind Him. For of two objects, either may be said to be removed from the other: the object that remains may be said to be removed from the one that goes away, and the one that goes away may be said to be removed from the one that remains. Besides, Matthew has indicated most clearly that He did indeed pray that the cup might pass from Him, but yet that His request was that this should take place not as He willed, but as the Father willed it. The words given by Mark and Luke, again, ought to be introduced in their proper connection. For Mark says, "Nevertheless not what I will, but what Thou wilt;" and Luke says, "Nevertheless not my will, but Thine be done." He did then express Himself to that effect, and He did desire that His passion might abate and reach its end speedily. But it was the Father's will at the same time that He should carry out His conflict in a manner demanding sustained effort, and in sufficient measure. Accordingly He (the Father) adduced all that assailed Him. But of the missiles that were hurled against Him, some were shivered in pieces, and others were dashed back as with invulnerable arms of steel, or rather as from the stern and immoveable rock. Blows, spitting, scourgings, death, and the lifting up in that death, all came upon Him; and when all these were gone through, He became silent and endured in patience unto the end, as if He suffered nothing, or was already dead. But when His death was being prolonged, and when it was now overmastering Him, if we may so speak, beyond His utmost strength, He cried out to His Father, "Why hast Thou forsaken me?" And this exclamation was in due accordance with the requests He had previously made: Why is it that death has been in such close conjunction with me all along up till now, and Thou dost not yet bear the cup past me? Have I not drank it already, and drained it? But if not, my dread is that I may be utterly consumed by its continuous pressure; and that is what would befall me, wert Thou to forsake me: then would the fulfilment abide, but I would pass away, and be made of none effect. Now, then, I entreat Thee, let my baptism be finished, for indeed I have been straitened greatly until it should be accomplished.—This I judge to have been the Savior's meaning in this concise utterance. And He certainly spoke truth then. Nevertheless He was not forsaken. Albeit He drank out the cup at once, as His plea had implied, and then passed away. And the vinegar which was handed to Him seems to me to have been a symbolic thing. For the turned wine indicated very well the quick turning and change which He sustained when He passed from His passion to impassibility, and from death to deathlessness, and from the position of one judged to that of one judging, and from subjection under the despot's power to the exercise of kingly dominion. And the sponge, as I think, signified the complete transfusion of the Holy Spirit that was realized in Him. And the reed symbolized the royal scepter and the divine law. And the hyssop expressed that quickening and saving resurrection of His by which He has also brought health to us. But we have gone through these matters in sufficient detail on Matthew and John. With the permission of God, we shall speak also of the account given by Mark. But at present we shall keep to what follows in our passage.

IV.—An Exposition of Luke XXII. 46, Etc.

This prayer He also offered up Himself, falling repeatedly on His face; and on both occasions He urged

His request for not entering into temptation: both when He prayed, "If it be possible, let this cup pass from me;" and when He said, "Nevertheless not as I will, but as Thou wilt." For He spoke of not entering into temptation, and He made that His prayer; but He did not ask that He should have no trial whatsoever in these circumstances, or that no manner of hardship should ever befall Him. For in the most general application it holds good, that it does not appear to be possible for any man to remain altogether without experience of ill: for, as one says, "The whole world lieth in wickedness;" and again, "The most of the days of man are labor and trouble," as men themselves also admit. Short is our life, and full of sorrow. Howbeit it was not meet that He should bid them pray directly that that curse might not be fulfilled, which is expressed thus: "Cursed is the ground in thy works: in sorrow shalt thou eat of it all the days of thy life;" or thus, "Earth thou art, and unto earth shalt thou return." For which reason the Holy Scriptures, that indicate in many various ways the dire distressfulness of life, designate it as a valley of weeping. And most of all indeed is this world a scene of pain to the saints, to whom He addresses this word, and He cannot lie in uttering it: "In the world ye shall have tribulation." And to the same effect also He says by the prophet, "Many are the afflictions of the righteous." But I suppose that He refers to this entering not into temptation, when He speaks in the prophet's words of being delivered out of the afflictions. For He adds, "The Lord will deliver him out of them all." And this is just in accordance with the Savior's word, whereby He promises that they will overcome their afflictions, and that they will participate in that victory which He has won for them. For after saying, "In the world ye shall have tribulation," He added, "But be of good cheer, I have overcome the world." And again, He taught them to pray that they might not fall into temptation, when He said, "And lead us not into temptation;" which means, "Suffer us not to fall into temptation." And to show that this did not imply they should not be tempted, but really that they should be delivered from the evil, He added, "But deliver us from evil." But perhaps you will say, What difference is there between being tempted, and falling or entering into temptation? Well, if one is overcome of evil—and he will be overcome unless he struggles against it himself, and unless God protects him with His shield—that man has entered into temptation, and is in it, and is brought under it like one that is led captive. But if one withstands and endures, that man is indeed tempted; but he has not entered into temptation, or fallen under it. Thus Jesus was led up of the Spirit, not indeed to enter into temptation, but "to be tempted of the devil." And Abraham, again, did not enter into temptation, neither did God lead him into temptation, but He tempted (tried) him; yet He did not drive him into temptation. The Lord Himself, moreover, tempted (tried) the disciples. And thus the wicked one, when he tempts us, draws us into the temptations, as dealing himself with the temptations of evil; but God, when He tempts (tries), adduces the temptations as one untempted of evil. For God, it is said, "cannot be tempted of evil." The devil, therefore, drives us on by violence, drawing us to destruction; but God leads us by the hand, training us for our salvation.

V.—On John VIII.12.

Now this word "I am" expresses His eternal subsistence. For if He is the reflection of the eternal light, He must also be eternal Himself. For if the light subsists forever, it is evident that the reflection also subsists forever. And that this light subsists, is known only by its shining; neither can there be a light that does not give light. We come back, therefore, to our illustrations. If there is day, there is light; and if there is no such thing, the sun certainly cannot be present. If, therefore, the sun had been eternal, there would also have been endless day. Now, however, as it is not so, the day begins when the sun rises, and it ends when the sun sets. But God is eternal light, having neither beginning nor end. And along with Him there is the reflection, also without beginning, and everlasting. The Father, then, being eternal, the Son is also eternal, being light of light; and if God is the light, Christ is the reflection; and if God is also a Spirit, as it is written, "God is a Spirit," Christ, again, is called analogously Spirit.

VI.—Of the One Substance.

The plant that springs from the root is something distinct from that whence it grows up; and yet it is of one nature with it. And the river which flows from the fountain is something distinct from the fountain. For we cannot call either the river a fountain, or the fountain a river. Nevertheless we allow that they are both one according to nature, and also one in substance; and we admit that the fountain may be conceived of as father, and that the river is what is begotten of the fountain.

VII.—On the Reception of the Lapsed to Penitence

But now we are doing the opposite. For whereas Christ, who is the good *Shepherd*, goes in quest of one who wanders, lost among the mountains, and calls him back when he flees from Him, and is at pains to take him up on His shoulders when He has found him, we, on the contrary, harshly spurn such a one even when He approaches us. Yet let us not consult so miserably for ourselves, and let us not in this way be driving the sword against ourselves. For when people set themselves either to do evil or to do good to others, what they do is certainly not confined to the carrying out of their will on those others; but just as they attach themselves to iniquity or to goodness, they will themselves become possessed either by divine virtues or by unbridled passions. And the former will become the followers and comrades of the good angels; and both in this world and in the other, with the enjoyment of perfect peace and immunity from all ills, they will fulfil the most blessed destinies unto all eternity, and in God's fellowship they will be forever (in possession of) the supreme good. But these latter will fall away at once from the peace of God and from peace with themselves, and both in this world and after death they will abide with the spirits of blood-guiltiness. Wherefore let us not thrust from us those who seek a penitent return; but let us receive them gladly, and number them once more with the steadfast, and make up again what is defective in them.

Note by the American Editor.

Frequent references to *Gallandi*, whose collection I have been unable to inspect, the cost of the best edition being about two hundred dollars, makes it worthwhile to insert here, from a London book-catalogue, the following useful memoranda: *"Gallandii, Cong. Orat.* (Andr.) Bibliotheca Veterum Patrum Antiquorumque Scriptorum Ecclesiasticorum Græco- Latina; Opera silicet eorundum minora ac rariora usque ad xiii. Sæculum complexa, quorum clxxx. et amplius nec in Veteri Parisiensi, neque in postrema Lugdunensi edits sunt. Venet., 1765.

"The contents are given in Darling, col. 298–306. Of the three hundred and eighty-nine writers enumerated, it appears that nearly two hundred are not in the earlier collections.

"The contents of these great collections are, not the works of the Great Fathers, of whose writings separate editions have been published, but the works, often extensive and important, of those numerous Ecclesiastical writers whose works go, with the Greater Fathers referred to, to make up the sum of Church Patristic literature."

Find this and other great works of the early Church Fathers at lighthousechristianpublishing.com.

Our Father who art in heaven, hallowed be
thy name.
Thy kingdom come, Thy will be done, on
earth as it is in heaven.
Give us this day our daily bread and
forgive us our trespasses as we forgive those who
trespass against us.
And lead us not into temptation, but deliver
us from evil, for Thy is the kingdom, the power
and the glory.

Amen

Hail Mary full of grace, the Lord is with thee. Blessed art thou amongst women and blessed is the fruit of thy womb Jesus. Holy Mary mother of God, pray for us sinners, now and the hour of our death.

www.ingramcontent.com/pod-product-compliance
Lightning Source LLC
Chambersburg PA
CBHW050225100526
44585CB00017BA/2017